EDITH STEIN –
WOMAN OF PRAYER

EDITH STEIN – WOMAN OF PRAYER

HER LIFE AND IDEALS

Joanne Mosley

GRACEWING

First published in 2004

Gracewing
2 Southern Avenue, Leominster
Herefordshire
HR6 0QF

© Joanne Mosley 2004

ISBN 0 85244 596 2

Typeset by Action Publishing Technology Ltd,
Gloucester GL1 5SR

CONTENTS

PROLOGUE

It was Sunday morning, just before ten o'clock. It was also the moment of my very first talk on Edith Stein. As I looked at the mass of expectant faces, I began to speak: 'Today, Edith Stein is being canonized.'

It was 11 October 1998. At that very moment, thousands of people were crowded into St Peter's Square. But far away, in a long, narrow room in a quiet corner of Oxfordshire, Rome's new saint was possibly still only a name. So I began to introduce Edith Stein. But where to begin? Edith is famous for so many things that there is always the danger of just reeling off a formidable list of labels: Jewess and philosopher, convert and writer, lecturer and feminist, Carmelite nun and victim of Auschwitz. Even after her death, the list has continued to grow: saint and martyr, co-patroness of Europe; and it has already been suggested that she could become Doctor of the Church. But to my mind, there is one label that holds all the others together, that I feel is the essence of Edith Stein: she was, first and foremost, *a woman of prayer*.

In the midst of the world, Edith carried with her a radiant inner life wherever she went. At home, in the classroom, socializing with friends, or inspiring her lecture audiences. Immediately after her conversion, Edith had wanted to enter Carmel; in fact, it was another twelve years before her dream came true. But in that time, she deepened her understanding of the link between prayer and the world, and passed on her insights to others. As she wrote to a friend in 1928, six years after becoming a Catholic:

> Immediately before, and for a good while after my conversion, I was of the opinion that to lead a religious life meant one had to give up all that was secular and to live totally immersed in thoughts of the Divine. But gradually I realized that something else is asked of us in this world and that, even in the contemplative life, one may not sever the connection with the world. I even believe that the deeper one is drawn into God, the more one must 'go out of oneself'; that is, one must go to the world in order to carry the divine life into it.

Edith, I always feel, had that special something to offer the world. Not that she was aware of any influence of her own. I once heard it said that virtue is like perfume: the wearer cannot smell it but everybody else can! Edith, so inspiringly calm to others, could well see her own human need: 'Women's souls,' she once said, 'are in commotion so much'. If we think that her prayer was only ever the heights of contemplation or burning intercession, then we are wrong. It was also her basic survival technique for getting through the daily grind: a schedule that began around dawn and went on till nearly midnight. She remembered the panic on waking up in the morning. How to fit everything in? Then Edith would stop and say to herself: 'Take it easy! Not any of this may touch me now. My first morning's hour belongs to the Lord.'

This, I believe, is the key to all her prayer: total absorption in God that is able to shut out worries, memories, even surroundings. As she advised in that same letter of 1928:

> The only essential is that one finds, first of all, a quiet corner in which one can communicate with God as though there were nothing else, and that must be done daily.

The effects of her prayer are breathtaking. When I feel most in need of inspiration, I go back again and again to the accounts of Edith in Westerbork concentration camp. The setting must have been dreadful to behold: barbed wire, watchtowers, soldiers with machine guns, ugly barrack blocks, and everywhere faces etched with misery and fear. And then, for one eyewitness, Edith came into the picture; and as she was speaking to him, he felt he was 'journeying into another world, where for the moment, Westerbork ceased to exist.' Edith Stein, this woman whom he described as 'walking, talking, and praying ... like a saint', was so radiant with the presence of God that she was again shutting out surroundings – this time for other people. In a world of hatred and confusion, she was a visible sign of love.

A woman of prayer, Edith was also a person of *ideals*. This did not stop her from being a realist – her feet on the ground, objective, seeking only the truth. But realism needs ideals: without them, we risk setting our sights too low. Edith followed ideals like guiding stars: the truth, the Cross, sacrifice as fullness of love. Along with these ideal 'things' were ideal 'figures': beginning with Jesus, whose image she held 'continually before her eyes', then the Virgin Mary, Queen Esther, and the saints of Carmel. They were landmark figures who played an indispensable role in Edith's life and prayer: they brought out of her something that was already there and gave it back to her in an enriched form. To them she owed so much. I, too, owe so much to Edith Stein. For her integrity and love, strength and compassion, sparkling humour and heartfelt joy – for the whole person who is 'Edith'.

I owe a great deal to other people, too. There is Sr Paula Coulbois, OSB, whom I met in Orléans in 1992: the first person who ever spoke to me of Edith Stein. As a result, I attended a retreat on Edith where I had the good fortune to meet Pat Lyne, OCDS, now author of the biography *Edith Stein Discovered*; Pat shared with me some of her long-standing love and enthusiasm for her. My sincere thanks are also due to Fr Matt Blake, OCD and to all those since who have invited me to speak on Edith; likewise to the many listeners: their contributions in discussion have invariably been interesting and enriching. Finally, it is a pleasure to express my gratitude to three particular sources of help to me over the years: to the German Edith Stein Society, prolific with the latest information on matters concerning Edith; to Sandra Pooley, who has stocked the Carmelite Book Service in Oxford with all the German works by and on Edith Stein that I could ever dream of having; and to my mother, who has patiently typed the final draft of this book and been, at the same time, a most exacting and insightful critic.

Part I
Ideals in Edith's Life

CHAPTER ONE

THE SEARCH FOR THE TRUTH

'God is truth. All who seek truth seek God, whether this is clear to them or not.'[1]

These words of Edith Stein's were written in hindsight, years after her conversion. They also point to what was central in her life, the passion of her life: truth, and the search for the truth. This passion was even to become imprinted on her whole person. In Westerbork concentration camp, for example, an official she met felt prompted to call her 'so whole and honest and genuine'.[2] He could also have said: she loved the truth.

What gave Edith, right from her childhood, a love of truth? It was not religion. Even though she came from a devout family, an observant Jewish family, it was not there that she found the truth. Rather like many cradle Catholics, there was a barrier to be climbed, indeed a gate closed, before she could spring over it and come face to face with the truth. Not that Judaism did not give her what she called her 'high moral heritage'[3] and sense of ideals. But to be Jewish meant mostly for the young Edith being part of a huge family network. As a child, she mastered certain mnemonics for learning the names of the twelve sons of Jacob. Then she had to do the same to memorize the names of her relations: aunts and uncles alone numbered thirty-seven!

There were also the Jewish festivals: the Passover, the New Year and others, especially the Day of Atonement – the highest holy day in Judaism, the day on which Edith was born in 1891, a feast which she kept as her own long after she had lost her childhood faith. Her father had died when she was not yet two, and that left Auguste Stein, who would prove herself truly a strong woman in the Jewish tradition of the *mulier fortis*, the matriarch of the family who brought up seven children and turned the floundering timber business left her by her husband into a lucrative enterprise. So, Siegfried Stein was dead, and it fell to Edith's brothers to read out the Passover prayers normally said by the father of the family. The brothers were not devout, they had little respect. No doubt their mother felt a wave of sadness. And Edith? She began to see that it was possible not to take religion seriously. How often in this way faith is relativized when other things seem more important. At school, we are told, Edith was indifferent to questions of religion.

We note that Edith still prayed. Much is made of the fact that she became an 'atheist' at the age of fifteen, when living with a sister in Hamburg. At that time, she tells us, she 'deliberately and consciously' gave up praying.[4] What that also tells us, though, is that she had been praying up to that time. Probably not a prayer of deep faith, and even more certainly not a fulfilment of her search for the truth.

When Edith returned home after ten months away from school, she set about returning to her studies. She had to apply herself. Edith was extremely bright but had to make up a lot of lost ground. She was also preparing for an entrance exam, so as to be taken into the higher levels of the school where she could study for university. The family business was thriving by now. Whereas elder brothers and sisters were working in it, helping the family to make ends meet from the time they left school, Auguste could now afford to put her two youngest through higher education – Edith and her sister Erna, two years her senior. They were given a pep talk by an uncle on the importance of a professional career, the guarantee of future security. In short, they should study medicine. Erna, who loved languages, saw 'reason' and agreed to study medicine; she became a very competent doctor later on. It was at this time that Edith dropped a bombshell: *she* wanted to study philosophy. The family were staggered, totally taken aback. How on earth had she come to that decision? (And what a useless prospect for the future!) Edith had read only one book on the subject, but she knew instinctively that that was her path. She wanted to study philosophy, she said later, because it was the surest path to the truth.

At Breslau University, Edith took not only philosophy but three other subjects as well: psychology, history and German literature. A sort of compromise. They were required for a teaching qualification, and it would please her family if at least she could become qualified in something. But they were not token subjects. With the enquiring mind that was Edith's, they opened up new realms of truth.

She became heavily involved in psychology, even considering doing research on it one day. She had found a whole buried area waiting to be uncovered – the truth of the human person, the mind and the consciousness. Then there was history. Edith had no intention of romanticizing about the past. She wanted to be part of 'history in the making'.[5] Her own studies would become the bedrock of her interest in politics. As a student at Breslau, she joined a suffragette movement, campaigning for the right of Prussian women to vote. So full was she of her ideals that she found herself despising those students who took no interest in the higher things of life. Walking into the lecture hall, she would turn her head away from them and think, 'The Idiots'![6] Edith was not yet a saint!

Finally, there was German literature. One could say that she was exposed to the truth here. She had to study the Gospel in medieval German but 'at that time it had no religious impact on me'.[7] Along with this came encounters with simple faith. Edith was a member of the League for School Reform, and for field trips the members would visit different institutions. Once, they went to a children's home run by Protestant deaconesses. We wanted a sewing machine, one of them told the group; so we prayed for one, and in due time the machine arrived. Edith listened to this account, which was given in all seriousness. Then she looked around at the other students, all of them 'free-thinkers', and noticed that not one was sceptical, not one was concealing a snigger or an embarrassed smile. She was impressed by the childlike faith of the sister, but as yet it was still eclipsed for her by the all-important notion of the truth.

This becomes crystal clear when Edith sank into weeks of depression. At first sight, she seems an unlikely depressive – this active, purposeful young woman with heaps of self-confidence, sporting a wealth of ideals like a string of pearls. That was part of the trouble. Reality has never been ideal. And if some literature contains powerful descriptions of the ideal – like the 'sublime' acceptance of death by Mary Stuart in the Schiller play that so inspired Edith – there is a whole bank of other literature that portrays life as worse than reality. Edith stumbled across one such book, Popert's novel, *Helmut Harringa*. She was perhaps drawn to it because it was all about student life. But what student life! Drinking, immorality – Edith sensed the presence of evil, and was frightened. It may also have seemed to her that her ideals were in vain. That maybe she was living in an illusory world that would never find a home in real life. She became profoundly depressed. Until, that is, she attended a concert. The music by Bach, the words of a hymn by Luther: 'truth will triumph through us'.[8] Edith caught these words and her crisis was over. Yes, she thought, if I and my friends all strive for the truth, evil will be conquered.

We switch now to a small room in the philosophy faculty at Breslau. It was just before Christmas 1912, Edith had been a student there for over eighteen months now. She had a pile of books on the table, books on the psychology of thought, and she was preparing a seminar paper. From time to time a name caught her eye, the seven letters making up the word, 'Husserl'. The authors she read were always referring to this name, like someone worth quoting.

The door opened. 'Mos,' she greeted the other student. His real name was Georg Moskiewicz, but everyone knew him as

'Mos'. He asked what she was working on. Edith pointed to the books piled on the table. 'Leave all that stuff aside,' he said, almost as an order. Edith was surprised. Mos then handed her a different book and told her to read it instead. The name printed on this one was 'Edmund Husserl'. The greatest philosopher of the day, Edith would soon find out. The founder of 'Phenomenology', a new movement in philosophy that strove to find the truth. Mos had actually studied under the great man himself, in Göttingen, and longed to return there. To that place where 'all you do [is] philosophize, day and night'.[9] Edith felt the excitement rising in her.

The room was empty now. The Christmas vacation. All the books had been put away except for that one, the one bearing Husserl's name: *Logical Investigations*, Volume Two. Edith was reading it with bated breath, for the book was airing the very same doubts that she herself had about her own studies of psychology. A science in its infancy, it used term after term and took them for granted. But there were no foundations, not one concept that anyone had defined. How, Edith would say, could a historian write about the 'State', about 'peoples', if no one had clarified the meaning of the words? How could a physicist speak of 'matter' and 'space' without someone investigating them first?[10] Still more to the point: how could psychologists refer to the 'mind', without exploring the essence of the mind, its truth?

Little did Edith know it at that time, but phenomenology was Catholic philosophy without the name. Husserl himself had been inspired by Thomas Aquinas who strove for truth, for essences. Since Thomas in the thirteenth century – and especially with the impetus of Descartes in the seventeenth – philosophy had gradually fallen away from valuing objective truth to approving subjective opinions, where everyone had his or her own idea and could give their own meaning to a thing.[11] Now, with Husserl, here was someone saying that you should look at things as they appear to you – hence the word, 'phenomena' ('appearances') – and believe not only that the truth about it was out there, but also that you could have access to it.

Edith kept her secret to herself. '*Secretum meum mihi*,' she would later say about her religious call and its conflicts, when she wanted to work them out in the intimacy of her own heart. Her 'call' to phenomenology – it cannot be spoken of in any other way – was her own most intimate secret at the present time. A vocation, it came true. One evening, she found a letter from her cousin Richard, now in Göttingen, who would happily welcome her if she wanted to study there. Edith announced her decision. For a second time, the family was dumbfounded. But she had her way and moved to the north German city in the spring of 1913.

To love the truth one must revere it and follow it wherever it leads. Edith was doing this, just by travelling to Göttingen. To love the truth one must have a mind that is unalloyed, single-minded, paying no attention to false gods, to ideals of honour and prestige. Edith's arrival in Göttingen shows this even more. It was the first week of term. She had bought Husserl's new book, *Ideas*, Volume One, that had just come out. She read it through – a feat in itself – and was disappointed. The ideal of objective truth that had shone out like a bright light from the pages of the first book was now fading, threatening to be smothered by the pages of the second. Edith was the first to arrive at Husserl's house where all his students were to gather. He was 'The Master', possibly the greatest living philosopher. She was a brand new student with nothing to her name beyond a school-leaving certificate. And she told him, without any qualms, that she was concerned about his most recent book. It did not spoil the relationship between them that would develop when she became his star student. But it could have done. Edith had come to Göttingen to work towards the truth, not to bask in the glory of working with a famous person, and she was fearless in defending the truth.

To tell the truth one needs gentleness. This was something Edith had yet to learn. She was only too aware of her tendency to 'criticize without reflecting at length whether [she had] a right to do so'.[12] In her circle of students were two staunch friends, Fritz Kaufmann and Hans Lipps. One day, Fritz wrote to her, hurt at her suggestion that she felt she understood Hans better than he did. Yes, she wrote back the same day, that is true! The 'offended' Fritz might have been glad if at that time she had known the words of Ephesians 4:15 – tell the truth, but with charity!

One needs immense courage to tell the truth. There is an outstanding episode which Edith relates in her autobiography, *Life in a Jewish Family*, but which is rarely quoted. She had interrupted her studies at Göttingen to train as a Red Cross nurse when the First World War broke out. She did a few months' stint in 1915, nursing sick soldiers in Austria. When leaving, she said goodbye to the patients and agreed to take their letters with her across the border, even though it was forbidden by censorship laws. She was challenged by customs officials and told to hand over the mail. Back home again, Edith was informed that she would have to face a military court. The best thing she could do would be to plead ignorance of the law. If not, she would most certainly be sent to prison. To the family's horror, Edith refused to lie. She protested she would rather go to prison than lie. As it happened, the Red Cross intervened on her behalf and the case was dropped. Had it gone ahead, this episode would be far better known in the life of Edith Stein!

One needs love, courage, determination, to follow the truth. Perhaps most of all, one needs humility. Edith, we must always remember, was a philosopher. A philosopher constructs a system of ideas. Sometimes the system excludes mention of God: after all, to bring God into one's neat, well-thought-out and, above all, *human* system of ideas can upturn the apple cart! Sometimes, philosophy is downright hostile to the notion of God. 'Philosophy' means 'love of wisdom', but that can also mean purely human wisdom. St Paul was not slow in pointing this out. Nor was a French priest who called by at the presbytery near Speyer where Edith, by then a Catholic, was a teacher. She, too, was visiting at that moment. When the guest learnt that she had studied philosophy, he exclaimed: 'Then I'm surprised you didn't lose your faith!' 'On the contrary,' she replied, 'I found it.'[13]

Philosophy can work for or against God, depending on the

view of wisdom one takes: true wisdom or purely human wisdom. Edith was looking for pure wisdom and for this reason she was humble when truth presented itself. She had begun in Göttingen to have respect for questions of faith. These were her own words. So many of her fellow students and even the most brilliant lecturers were committed Christians. Edith therefore realized that faith was a world which would have to be given due consideration. As she said, she made herself open to the stimuli around her, and without even noticing it, she was already being gradually transformed.

Open to stimuli. This is already humility: being shaped rather than shaping one's destiny. Now we recall that Edith Stein was a philosophical writer. She too was building up a system of ideas. She was writing a doctoral thesis which would be published under the title, *On the Problem of Empathy*. The 'problem' was whether and how it was possible to understand another person's experience, to slip into his or her skin like a hand in a glove. To examine this question, Edith gave a full analysis of the human person: starting with the body, then moving onto the mind. First, the part of it that is linked to the body, that feels hunger, thirst and so on, and which she called the 'soul'. Secondly, that part of the mind that she called the 'spirit': the part of us that has feelings, responds to values, relates to other people, and makes empathy possible.

And so Edith built up her philosophical outline of the human person, just like the doctor who can point to a model skeleton and tell you where every part is and how it fits into the whole. This was Edith's system of ideas. Then she began to be exposed to the notion of faith. Her love for the truth went along with humility. She therefore had to include religion in her system of ideas, or else her analysis would be incomplete. She put it in right at the end, as a kind of summit in her description of the spirit. But it was still a world closed to her. It must have cost her a lot, this conscientious and perceptive philosopher who was otherwise 'on top' of her subject, to finish her thesis with the words, 'It is not clear'. Later, many years later, when she was a Carmelite, Edith would be imbued with the writings of Teresa and Thérèse, two great Doctors of the Church who had taught that humility is truth and truth humility.

Edith obtained her doctorate with glowing colours in 1916 and moved to Freiburg where she became Husserl's assistant, revising and editing his own works and manuscripts. In these eighteen months or so, she became open to yet more stimuli. There was, for example, her first trip to Freiburg on the way to the oral examination. She broke the long journey by visiting Frankfurt, where a friend took her to the Cathedral. Only as a tourist. But while walking around it, she saw an ordinary-looking woman come in with her shopping basket and pray before the tabernacle. Edith probably did not know what the tabernacle was. But she did know that she was witnessing an 'intimate conversation'[14] with God – the very thing that would one day point her towards the definitive 'truth'. She never forgot this experience.

Her favourite lecturer was a committed Christian. Adolf Reinach had helped her many a time to come to grips with phenomenology at the beginning of her studies. By now, he was on the front, a soldier like so many, plucked out of civilized life and planted in the mud of the trenches.

Another Christmas vacation. It was the end of 1917, and Edith heard that Reinach had been killed in action. She was absolutely devastated. But she felt that for her there was almost worse to come. His widowed, beloved Anne would be even more crushed by grief, she felt. And Edith was going to meet her. She was dreading it, she didn't know what on earth she could say to console her.

On the day, it was completely different. Anne was visibly radiating strength from the depths of her sadness. From a death was shining a belief in the afterlife. Perhaps Anne had never seemed to Edith so strong, so supported by God as she appeared in those hours. It gave Edith a whole understanding of how one could be 'blessed by the Cross', not annihilated beneath it:

It was then that I first encountered the Cross and the divine strength which it inspires in those who bear it. For the first time I saw before my very eyes the Church, born of Christ's redemptive suffering, victorious over the sting of death. It was the moment in which my unbelief was shattered, Judaism paled, and Christ streamed out upon me: Christ in the mystery of the Cross.[15]

Faced with the *support* of suffering, when lived in the light of truth, Edith buckled under the weight of evidence. She decided to become a Christian.

We have seen that to follow the truth, one needs charity, courage, humility. And above all one needs to live it, to move forward, to follow the truth wherever it leads. But how was Edith to do this? She felt sure it was not enough just to think of herself as a Christian. She would have to take action, take steps, belong to a Church, and for Edith there was nothing drawing her to any particular Church, Protestant or Catholic. The way ahead was not clear. And for the first time, she found herself resisting truth.

There then began three, even four, very painful years. When she had survived them, when she could see clearly what was going on in them, she would look back and say that at that time her 'head and heart were at war'.[16] Her heart was Catholic but her head in confusion – unable and unwilling to make the decisions her heart required. And so she stagnated in frustration. Her health suffered, and she became so exhausted that she was in desperate need of rest. God's rest.

Edith was at home in her mother's house. She had not achieved the longed-for university post, for she was a woman, a Jewess; she had no contacts who would pull strings for her. So she was simply at home, an independent scholar. And here she had a glimpse of 'resting in God'. If there were only the will power, the jolt, one could make that very little jump from 'death' to 'life'. She now wrote:

There is a state of resting in God, an absolute break from all intellectual activity, when one forms no plans, makes no decisions and for the first time really ceases to act, when one simply hands over the future to God's will and 'surrenders himself to fate'. I myself have experienced this state to some extent. It came in the wake of an experience which had overtaxed my strength, drained my spiritual resources and robbed me of the ability to act. Compared to that inertia arising from a lack of vital energy, 'resting in God' is something entirely new and distinct. One is a kind of 'stillness of death', whereas the other is marked by a sense of tremendous security ... which, to the degree I give myself to it, fills me with life ... [17]

Filled with life. Yes, but the key words are 'to the degree I give myself to it'. Edith could still not make that vital move. And her health got worse. There was another Christmas vacation, 1920. She remembers this time as the wedding of her sister Erna, and how she thought she would never be able to join in. Edith was 'in so much pain that the slightest sound made me cringe'. This was 'as a result of the spiritual conflicts I then endured in complete secrecy and without any human support'.[18] *Secretum meum mihi.* Always the most intimate decisions, and troubles, she kept secret. She joined in the dancing – her doctor sister had given her a shot of morphine! But where was the spiritual morphine to come from, when would the pain end?

The widowed Anne Reinach had bought a book. An edition, that had just come out, of the autobiography of Teresa of Jesus. The saint from Avila. Anne and her husband, Adolf, had been baptized as Lutherans. We may wonder, therefore, why Anne would own such a book. No doubt because she had already decided to become a Catholic, as indeed had Adolf just before his death.[19] So, the book was sitting in her library. Teresa of Avila.

Edith had made a journey. She had spent a few days with Anne on her way to visit Hatti – Husserl's other female star pupil, Hedwig Conrad-Martius. We can picture the scene. Anne offered Edith a book from her library as she was leaving. She looked around and chose – a reddish-brown cover and gold lettering on the front: 'Teresa of Jesus'. Edith took it with her to Hatti's, gave it to her as a present. It was only read when Hatti and her husband were going away for a while.[20]

Edith took the book upstairs and began to read. She devoured each word of the forty chapters, one after the other. Teresa telling her life. Her desire to follow God. Her miserable beginnings. Her longing for prayer, her laziness and ingratitude in giving up praying, after so many graces. A relentless unfolding of her life, unsparing of her faults. Her encounter with the God who suffered so much for us. Her intimate relationship with him. (Would Edith have thought of the woman in Frankfurt Cathedral?) And then, chapter forty, the summit: Christ revealing himself as the Truth.

Edith put the book down. Dawn comes early in the southern German summers. But the golden rays peeping through the shutters were nothing in comparison to the treasure she had found. 'That is the truth!' said Edith.

What is the truth? But we are asking the wrong question. It is not a *what*, it is a *Who*. Truth is a person, the person of Jesus. That is what Edith had been looking for and had failed to find in her books, libraries, seminars. Because truth is a person and not an intellectual concept. And because Teresa, she would say, said it all so truthfully.

Edith could now respond to the challenge of becoming a Christian. She did not go to bed at all but waited for the bookshop to open. She bought a catechism and a Catholic missal and began to prepare herself for being received into the Church, a step she would take on New Year's Day, 1922.

At fifteen, Edith had given up 'praying'. Or so she thought. But when she later considered whether she had prayed during all this time, she said: 'My longing for truth was a prayer in itself.'[21]

Notes

1   S-P, Letter 259, p. 272. (*See* pp. 152–4 for a list of abbreviations.) Edith is speaking about the imminent death of the philosopher, Husserl.

2   Herbstrith, *Edith Stein: A Biography*, p. 186. Although eyewitness accounts are from Westerbork, Edith died at Auschwitz.

3   ESGA 2, Letter 214, p. 227.
4   LJF, p. 148.
5   *Ibid.*, p. 190.
6   *Ibid.*, p. 191.
7   *Ibid.*, p. 190.
8   *Ibid.*, p. 216.
9   *Ibid.*, p. 218.
10 PPC, p. 8.
11 *See* Gosebrink, especially pp. 61–2.
12 S-P, Letter 32a, p. 39.
13 Feldes, *Edith Stein und Schifferstadt*, p. 46.
14 LJF, p. 401.
15 Posselt, p. 59.
16 *See* ESGA 4, Letter 94, p. 166.
17 From *Psychic Causality* (written 1918–1919); quoted here from Herbstrith, *Edith Stein: A Biography*, p. 60.
18 LJF, p. 237.
19 This information was supplied by Jan Nota, SJ, in his talk at the Seattle Regional Congress, 23 August 1987: reproduced on his cassette, *Blessed Edith Stein: 'A Woman of the Church'* (side 1). Anne became a Catholic in 1923, the year after her sister-in-law, Pauline Reinach.
20 This version of events, including Anne's ownership of the book, has only recently come to light: *see* ESGA 3, Letter 294, p. 27, n. 6 and Feldes, *Diesen lieben Blick*, pp. 8–9.
21 Posselt, p. 64.

CHAPTER TWO

THE TRUTH OF THE CROSS

It was the first day of the year, 1922. Edith stood at the baptismal font in the small parish church of Bergzabern. She was wearing the white wedding mantle of her godmother and best friend, Hatti. Her baptismal names were pronounced: Theresia Hedwig.[1] Teresa: the author of the *Life*. Hedwig: the friend in whose house she had read it. Both of them converging, setting the scene for Edith's conversion. And her discovery: that truth is a person, the person of Christ. She was now to find that truth was a person on the Cross.

The Cross was never far from Edith's path. There had been the overwhelming joy of her conversion. Followed almost immediately by a nagging worry: about how to break the news at home.[2] She was, she knew, extremely close to her mother, yet she half-expected to be thrown out and disowned. A Jew who left the faith was no longer a Jew[3] – maybe even cut off from the family. To her relief, this did not happen. Yet far worse, in Edith's eyes, were the harrowing tears of her rock-strong mother. As Edith would write: 'The *new self* carries the wounds of Christ'.[4]

Welcomed home by her bewildered family, Edith was still living with them in Breslau. But she felt in exile. She was a woman with a new life, yet totally surrounded by the old. Then, after a year, in the spring of 1923, there came a letter for her, through a Canon Joseph Schwind of Speyer. It was the solution to her problems.

Edith had met Schwind the previous February at her confirmation. To her delight, he agreed to be her spiritual director and they stayed in touch. He was an extraordinary person, quite as determined as Edith herself. When a boy, he had been noticed by the local curate who recognized his abilities and wanted to help. He gave him books: Latin, the language of the Church, perhaps to encourage a priestly vocation. But his father was not at all learned. In fact, Markus Schwind so hated learning that he snatched the books off his young son and threw them into the fire. He told Joseph in no uncertain terms to learn a practical trade instead. So Joseph took up 'carpentry'. He built a secret hiding place perched in a pear tree in the garden: his new library! His father was seemingly satisfied, and meanwhile the curate gave Joseph all the books he needed.[5] At the age of twenty-four, Joseph was ordained priest.

When the now 'Canon Schwind' met Edith Stein, he was seventy years old, the authoritarian Vicar-General who issued rules of conduct for visits to his house! Edith, though, received great kindness from him as he considered all her concerns, the main one being when and how to enter Carmel. On this point, Schwind was adamant: it was – for now – out of the question. Firstly, because of her mother. Secondly, because she had no experience of religious life. That was why the letter was so important. He had found her a teaching post at a convent school in Speyer.

A school run by nuns! That, wrote Edith excitedly, was 'the main point of attraction'.[6] It was a huge old school, joined to the convent which housed a hundred and seventy-nine Dominican nuns. It was a monastic life, with the sisters enclosed. Edith, the only non-enclosed teacher of a main subject – she mostly taught German language and literature – wanted to be as close to the community as possible. She lived in the gatehouse just outside the enclosure, usually wore clothes of black and white (the Dominican colours) and was delighted with her tiny room: 'I have never been so happy anywhere else before'.[7] She felt her heart leaping just to catch sight of the chapel tower. She was, she wrote ecstatically, 'living . . . like a real nun'.[8]

Had Edith forgotten her call to Carmel? Not in the least. But now, strangely, it didn't matter. Or maybe not so strangely. She was a new convert, carrying with her the ardour of her conversion. In the past eighteen months, it was as though time had been frozen. Her new life in Christ was, so to speak, put on hold – insofar as it was led in an environment where it had to be kept as discreet as possible, as though it did not exist, so as not to hurt anyone's feelings. In Breslau, Edith would leave the house at half past five, creep out of the front door and head towards St Michael's Church for the first Mass of the morning. She did not know it, but her mother always heard the door click and was filled with sadness. Then Edith appeared back for breakfast as though she had just got out of bed.

Here, in the convent at Speyer, was a convert's paradise! The chapel with the Blessed Sacrament, which Edith visited for an hour in the morning, for minutes snatched between lessons, and for up to several hours during the night! It softened her character, made her self-controlled, speaking from depths she never knew she had. There was the morning Mass, the offices throughout the day, the choir sisters who were her colleagues in the school, and the extern sisters whom Edith courageously helped in the kitchen, despite her pitiful menial skills. There was the prayer life of the Church, the different seasons of the liturgy, and the Dominican breviary from which Edith translated eighteen Latin hymns for those sisters who could not understand the original. There were the nuns to whom she gave extra tuition and whom she got to know best of all: Sr Callista, Sr Agnella. And finally, the huge shield above the entrance door: 'Veritas', 'The Truth'. The motto of the Dominican Order. And surely the motto of Edith Stein.

Alongside this wealth of experience remained the teaching. 'Not a labour of love,'[9] writes one author, from the school, while still recounting that Edith was a most outstanding teacher. No, Edith felt more called to the chapel than to the classroom, but what a teacher she was! She met everyone at the level they were at. She nurtured the shy and struggling, and promptly deflated the proud! She was an example of the line of John's Gospel, 'the truth will make you free' (8:32). People's opinions mattered little to her, just so long as she followed her conscience, and that is why she was so free and balanced and in control. A reproving silence was fearful to misbehaving girls, who wished they could disappear through a hole in the floor. Yet in the staff room, she was just as likely to plead on the girls' behalf. In fact, she was always standing up for them – except that they didn't know it! But they knew that she cared about them and they could tell her anything. As one pupil said: Edith Stein came there to teach them German, but in reality 'she ... gave us everything'.[10] Like Thérèse of Lisieux who taught her novices by instinct, so Edith taught in the way that was natural for her: she lectured, and she enthused everyone; she inspired just by the person she was.

If a reluctant teacher, Edith was, however, keen to learn. She steeped herself in every aspect of Catholic life. One person who suffered for this was Canon Schwind. He received Edith every Sunday, for hours at a time. His housekeeper and niece describes how, after one such meeting, he fell into a chair in the kitchen, wringing his hands and declaring: 'Oh, this philosopher! She can ask more questions than ten learned theologians could answer.'[11]

Schwind introduced Edith to the Jesuit and philosopher of religion, Erich Przywara. Through him, she began to study Thomas Aquinas in earnest – *the* Catholic philosopher.[12] She translated his work, *On Truth*, from Latin into German. The title could not be more perfect for Edith, but we must remember that it took its name from the first topic treated in the book. There were twenty-eight others, and this wide-ranging work took her into the heart of the thought of Aquinas. The effect on Edith cannot be underestimated. Because through this project she came to realize 'that it is possible to worship God by doing scholarly research'.[13] She had thought that she had to fill her mind exclusively with God. And so, she had given up philosophy after her conversion. She was now becoming her true self again. 'Living like a real nun' and also living like the real Edith Stein. Living in the truth.

17 September 1927. A date Edith never forgot: the sudden death of Canon Schwind. He had been hearing confessions in the Cathedral when he was suddenly taken ill. The penitent got up to call for help, but was called back by Schwind: 'You haven't received absolution yet.' After giving it, the Canon collapsed and was carried home, where he died during the last rites.[14] News reached Edith fast. She went straight to the house and kept watch by the body. And what, now, did she do on Sundays? From now on, Sunday was a visit to his grave.

We use the word, 'Cross', for many sufferings, and the loss of the Canon would have ranked as a big one for Edith. But there was a new impetus in her life that kept her moving on and not looking back. Her name began to be known in Catholic circles – she was the *Fräulein Doktor* at the school, the lady working on Thomas Aquinas, the published writer. Gradually, she was asked to write articles, to give talks.

Edith spoke a great deal for teachers. Women's education should be just that: education tailored for women. Not that she meant purely domestic subjects, but an emphasis on the arts, '*emotionally formative* subjects',[15] that brought the best out of the female mind. That meant, of course, defining what the female mind was. She was treading on controversial ground. Recent modes of thinking fell roughly into two groups: the people who believed that women should be wives and mothers and stay at the kitchen sink; and others who declared, on the contrary, that women were just the same as men. Edith's vision cut right through the two. She turned to Scripture, to Eve before the Fall: the ideal of womanhood in the mind of God. Woman, Edith felt, was indeed destined to be a wife and mother, but in a spiritual sense. She could and should do the jobs that men do but – and here Edith was categorical – woman is *not* the same as man. In an office, a factory, or even in parliament, woman will continue to be a wife and mother: a 'wife', in standing by a person's side; a 'mother', by helping others to develop and grow. It was not hard for Edith to stand up and speak. In Salzburg, the audience was a sea of faces – one thousand faces. She spoke compellingly for an hour and a half, without notes. This talk in particular, on 1 September 1930, really made Edith's name. It was followed by an avalanche of invitations to speak. Added to 'mountains of essays' to correct, it all became too big a burden for her. She was already sitting up working every night.

But now back to April 1928. The Canon had been dead for six months, and Edith decided to spend Easter at the Benedictine Abbey at Beuron. She made an appointment to see the Archabbot. Raphael Walzer, only three years older than Edith, an educated man with much experience of spiritual life, was immediately impressed. He found her so balanced and profound, a living embodiment of prayer. He was pleased to accept her request for him to become her new spiritual director. Eagerly, Edith spoke of her desire to enter Carmel. And then it was like coming up against a brick wall. Walzer would not hear of it. Nor had the Canon at first, but now she had the necessary experience of religious life. Archabbot Raphael, however, had a new objection to make: she was an important figure in the Catholic world, far too 'effective'[16] to shut herself away in a convent. Edith returned to Beuron the next Easter, but his response was just the same.

A vocation to the Cross is never mere words. It has to be lived before it is understood. That call was inherent in Edith, planted in her like the germ of her very self. And for a seed, pushing its way through the earth towards the light is never easy. In a human being, it is a painful process. For Edith, it was as though a light had been switched off. What, then, had gone wrong?

It was not only the attitude of Walzer. Edith was thirty-eight years old. She had been a Catholic for seven of them and worked with the Dominicans for the last six. She had been so fully involved, so brimming with life, so much a pillar of the school. She was inundated with school work, taking on more and more duties in her free time. Meanwhile, the public lectures were so demanding and so frequent that she was grinding herself into a state of exhaustion. And if she had no future as a Dominican ..., then what was she doing still there? When she had arrived at St Magdalena's six years ago, carrying her suitcase through the arch marked, 'Veritas', she had felt that she was exactly 'like a real nun'. Now, surely, it must have crossed her mind that the most important word was '*like*'. She was, she would say later, intimately involved in the convent but would never have dreamed of entering there.[17] Perhaps she felt she had only been playing at being a nun. But what caused her sudden change of mind?

There is a curious footnote, often glossed over or ignored, in the first biography written on Edith Stein. The author is her novice mistress at Cologne and she writes, possibly still quoting from a Dominican sister's report: 'Edith Stein asked to be admitted to the Carmel *Janua Coeli* in Würzburg but was refused.'[18] No date is given, but there are clues.

Two of the Dominicans, Edith's former pupils, Callista and Agnella, were taking further studies in Würzburg. Edith went to stay with them for Christmas 1929. They visited the Carmel together and attended the offices there. And when Edith got back to Speyer, she wrote what is possibly her worst-ever letter! It was to Roman Ingarden, her philosopher friend who was a reluctant Catholic. Edith was always writing to him – warmly, with encouragement, trying to bridge the gap between the strength of her belief and the tepidity of his own. But now, she was writing from a tightly locked fortress, with a big 'Keep Out' notice on the front door. You want to call me by an endearing term? Well, no you can't. 'There is something of family warmth about [it], and that has no place in my life any more. You must always think that there are invisible cell walls around me.'[19] This unfriendly letter – so different from the subtle warmth of her usual style – surely reveals a huge disappointment. The more her goal is out of reach, the more she is asserting it: fiercely, rigidly. There is no doubt about the nature of her frustration. The next month, she was writing to a Benedictine nun. She signed it, 'with best wishes and in longing for monastic life'.[20] But she was already living the monastic life, one might reply. Yes, but not in Carmel.

At the end of 1930, Edith made up her mind to resign from

schoolteaching. She left Speyer at the end of the following spring term. Not for Carmel but for her talks and for academia. Her monastic ideal still out of the question, she was preparing another thesis. Applying for a university lectureship all over again – twelve years after her first batch of unsuccessful attempts. She developed her work on Aquinas and set her sights on Freiburg. Even though Husserl had retired, Edith knew his successor.

The following December. Not another rigid letter but a cry from the depths: 'all is shrouded in darkness.'[21] These are the starkest words from Edith about her own dark night. Her application to Freiburg had failed, for economic reasons. Not that it would matter to her much if she could go after her true goal instead. But she could not, and it seemed to her that there was nothing. In fact, something did emerge. A teaching post at Münster in Northern Germany, at the main Catholic institute for education. It was back to the drawing board: studying the theory of education, a subject not her own by training. Edith would sometimes observe her colleagues, their absorption in their work, their dedication, and marvel at it with admiration.

There is almost nothing worse in employment than not having one's heart in it. There is a deep longing in everyone to belong, to be part of the team, 'to give everything and to give oneself', to quote Thérèse of Lisieux. Edith tried, she worked, she was conscientious. But she still wrote to Hatti in desperation: 'I . . . am generally incompetent for this world.'[22] That is coded language. It really means: I belong to the 'kingdom that is not of this world'. But at Christmas 1932, something changed. The dark night lifted and took on the colour of dawn.

Two years previously, Edith had been giving a talk at Bendorf on the principles of women's education. In the audience, she noticed a quiet nun who did not contribute to the discussion.[23] Her name was Petra Brüning, an Ursuline sister from Dorsten. Now, through two other sisters in the Order, Edith was invited to spend Christmas there. She had an inkling that she and Mother Petra would get on well. But they got on far better than she could have imagined. Mother Petra believed in her vocation. The lightening effect on Edith shows just how much she had been kept down when no one around her had given her any encouragement: the spiritual director and the Carmel of Würzburg were two big enough reasons to be discouraged! But this quiet nun here, a teaching sister, looked at Edith and recognized that she was already a nun in spirit, with or without a habit. And she must have seen in her the future Carmelite as well. Edith left there, full of optimism. No longer does she speak of darkness but of things becoming more 'clear'.[24] A bright start for a new year.

1933. One of the most ill-fated dates in history, the year that Hitler came to power. In this year, Edith was no longer merely suffering a Cross; on the contrary, the Cross itself became her very vocation, the meaning of her life.

It was not only the year of Hitler. It was also the Jubilee Year, designated as such by Pope Pius XI because it was the nineteen-hundredth anniversary of the crucifixion of Jesus. It is quite chilling to think about: good and evil streaming in from opposite directions and converging over the world at one point in history. And within this, closely allied to this, Edith received her mission.

While still at Münster, she saw and heard on an almost daily basis an increasing hostility towards the Jews. It ranged from a bishop making dismissive remarks about them,[25] to frightening violence on the streets of Münster. And 'official' persecution began almost as soon as Hitler had taken power, on 30 January of that year.

Edith could see where it was all leading: to full-blown anti-semitism. She also – being more clear-sighted than the people around her – could foresee a persecution of the Catholics. 'First the Jews and then the Catholic Church,'[26] she had once remarked, when looking on at a nationalistic march. Those will be the targets of persecution, she had told her astonished friend, while the people of Speyer were jubilantly cheering a procession by the German army.

Now, it seemed even closer to coming true. Edith decided to visit the Pope to request an encyclical. She would alert him to the dangers, to both Jews and Catholics, which came from the Nazi regime. Ironically, the Jubilee Year itself quashed her plans: Pius XI was too busy to see her in a private audience. So she realized she would have to write to him instead. But even before she knew this, she looked ahead to this meeting with the Pope and felt that her action did not seem enough. It was not, she said, 'of the essence'.[27] That was an intuition which would turn out to be true but which she was hard put to to explain – for this kind of action 'suited my nature'.[28] She had always been a campaigner. As a student at Breslau, she had canvassed for women to vote. When she had not been given a university lectureship at Göttingen, she had written to the minister to demand that posts be made open to women – and she had succeeded. Now, when evil was threatening to strike, she was turning to the highest authority possible: the head of the Catholic Church. But still, she felt she had something extra to contribute. In the spring of 1933, it suddenly became clear. There are two revelations: insights which set the path of her future.

As Thérèse of Lisieux would say, 'Everything is a grace.' Even getting locked out of the house. Edith was banging on the door of her lodgings in Münster when a colleague came across her. He was out walking with his wife and they invited her home. Sitting, talking, they got around to politics. To the Germany of 1933. Her friend had read some American newspapers. They carried reports, he told her, of Nazi cruelties against the Jews. She listened in horrified silence, for once not daring to reveal her origins: certainly not out of cowardice but because she felt she would distress her hosts if they knew that she was Jewish. And while she was listening, she became convinced that it was all in God's hands and that she herself was destined to share the fate of the Jewish people:

> True, I had heard of rigorous measures against the Jews before. But now a light dawned in my brain that once again God had put a heavy hand upon His people and that the fate of this people would also be mine.[29]

This episode took place some time in Lent. Still in Lent, in Passion Week – the week that in Edith's time came before Holy Week – she left, as usual, to spend Easter at Beuron. She stopped off on the way, in Cologne, to spend the night with another Hedwig: 'Hede' Spiegel, a Jewish convert and Edith's own god-daughter. It was now Passion Thursday, 6 April 1933. Hede told her there was a service that evening at the Carmelite monastery. In this Jubilee Year of the Passion, everywhere there were talks on the Cross. And so they went to the Carmel – possibly Edith's first visit to her future home. And here, she received an intimation that is possibly the most important revelation of her life.

Edith was listening to the sermon. Then her mind began to wander, almost against her will, because she was being absorbed by something else. She entered into dialogue with Jesus. He asked her something and she agreed:

> I talked with the Saviour and told Him that I knew that it was His cross that was now being placed upon the Jewish people; that most of them did not understand this, but that those who did, would have to take it up willingly in the name of all. I would do that. He should only show me how. At the end of the service, I was certain that I had been heard. But what this carrying of the cross was to consist in, that I did not yet know.[30]

This is an absolutely vital happening, her willing acceptance of her vocation to the Cross. There is something strikingly genuine about her response. It is often all too easy to accept a particular mission that we have chosen for ourselves, that we ourselves think is right; then, when it involves suffering or hardship, to call it the 'Cross'. But Edith was accepting the Cross itself – the Cross naked and without direction. She had no idea what it would involve in reality, but she happily accepted it because it was a genuine call. And she gave it a sincere and unhesitating reply. As with Mary uttering her *fiat*, the outcome was immediate. For the very next day, while Edith was travelling on to Beuron, Hitler passed a law forbidding Jews to teach or to work in any of the civil service professions. As a result, she was now unemployed. But as yet, she did not know this.

There was a new meeting with Archabbot Raphael. Edith esteemed him highly and, as always, she followed his guidance and advice not to apply to Carmel – at least not yet – because she was too 'effective' in the Catholic world and because of her mother. But she asked him nonetheless what she should do when she was dismissed from the institute. Walzer thought this highly unlikely. Edith herself knew nothing about the latest law but was always clear-sighted about politics. One could say she had a knack of reading the signs of the times. After this meeting, Edith immersed herself in the Passion, death and Resurrection of Christ, living it with him in spirit as she always did in her Easter retreat.

On the day after she returned to Münster, the Principal broke the news about her job. Without a murmur, Edith said that she realized she would never again be able to work in Germany. He was surprised that this apparent recluse was informed about current affairs. Soon afterwards, she was offered a teaching job in South America. If Edith had accepted this, we might still have heard of her but only for her writings. But she did not accept the post. Far from it, she *could* not accept the post. The true depth of the revelations she had received now took over in the decisions of her life.

'The fate of this people would also be mine.' So, it was unthinkable that Edith could leave Germany now – to escape, with a lucky few, the eye of the storm. After taking this decision, it was only a short leap of the mind to reconsidering Walzer's objections to her entering Carmel. Too useful in the world as a lecturer: but she could no longer teach. And the blow to her mother: but wouldn't her mother rather have her in a convent in Germany than a school in South America where she would never see her again? Her decision was already made. And then confirmed, after a few hours before the Blessed Sacrament. A lesson in decision-making.

God's thoughts are not always our thoughts (cf. Isa. 55:8). But in this particular case, God's thoughts and Edith's thoughts did coincide. As she waited in prayer, she became convinced: it was now time to enter Carmel. Jesus had given his assent. Who would now refuse it?

She wrote again to Raphael Walzer. Fearless, now, because 'the walls that had stood in my way had crumbled.' They crumbled, just like that rigid inner fortress, the 'cell' in the letter to Ingarden that was keeping Edith locked within herself. Now it opened wide as she 'ran to Carmel like a child into its mother's arms'[31] – Walzer's own words when he had come to realize the truth of her vocation. But for now, he sent back the vital message: permission to apply.

Edith took immediate steps. An introduction was arranged through a friend in Cologne who knew the Carmelite community. Interviews, mixing the everyday and the profound. Could she sing? (Not very well.) And should she not stay in the world, where she could still accomplish so much? Edith's answer defines her whole vocation, her call to the Cross:

> It is not human activity that can help us, but the sufferings of Christ. To have a share in them is what I long for.[32]

Edith was accepted; soon, she wrote to Hatti: 'On this glorious Pentecost day . . . '[33] The night, for now, had vanished.

Truth led Edith to Carmel and the Cross. It was twelve years since her conversion, her encounter with Teresa and with Christ, the incarnate Truth. It was an invitation, like two people holding beckoning hands, waiting for her to join them. Teresa in Carmel and Christ on the Cross. The Truth was on the Cross.

Notes

1   'Theresia' for Teresa of Avila, as spelt in the baptismal register. 'Hedwig' (nickname: 'Hatti') for Hedwig Conrad-Martius.
2   Edith broke the news before her baptism: *see* ESGA 4, Letter 78, p. 143.
3   Susanne Batzdorff, in SEL, p. 117.
4   SC, p. 273.
5   Feldes, *Edith Stein und Schifferstadt*, pp. 10–11.

6   ESGA 4, Letter 84, p. 152.
7   *Ibid.*, Letter 84, p. 152.
8   S-P, Letter 38a, p. 47.
9   Herrmann, p. 73.
10 Posselt, p. 72.
11 Feldes, *Edith Stein und Schifferstadt*, p. 15.
12 Gosebrink, p. 61.
13 S-P, Letter 45, p. 54; the original, '*Gottesdienst*', means both 'worship' and 'service' of God.
14 Feldes, *Edith Stein und Schifferstadt*, pp. 17–18.
15 W, p. 136.
16 SEL, p. 19.
17 *Ibid.*, p. 21.
18 Posselt, p. 76.
19 ESGA 4, Letter 131, p. 205.
20 Cf. S-P, Letter 51, p. 59.
21 *Ibid.*, Letter 108, p. 107.
22 *Ibid.*, Letter 126, p. 126.
23 *See* the list of people present: ESGA 13, p. 239.
24 S-P, Letter 133, p. 132.
25 Edith objected to 'harsh and unjust' remarks by Bishop Sigismund Waitz in his writings on St Paul. *See* the discussion of her letter of 6 March 1932 in Herbstrith (ed.), *Never Forget*, p. 82; also, the full text of the letter (misdated as 6 August 1932): ESGA 2, Letter 214, p. 227.
26 Herbstrith, *Edith Stein: Jüdin und Christin*, p. 70.
27 SEL, p. 16.
28 *Ibid.*, p. 16.
29 *Ibid.*, p. 16.
30 *Ibid.*, p. 17.
31 Posselt, p. 153.
32 Pohl, p. 66.
33 S-P, Letter 143, p. 144.

CHAPTER THREE

BLESSED BY THE CROSS

Edith was told to keep quiet about it. Not to tell the other sisters that she was Jewish. The novice mistress thought it best that way. But, Edith replied, looking at Mother Renata in astonishment: 'my sisters must be able to share my joys and sorrows, and must know that I am Jewish.'[1] Of course she knew, the new postulant, not to boast about her past, her studies, her career. But to hide the fact that she was Jewish – that would be like hiding herself. A Jewess in a Catholic convent: a sign of contradiction?

At home also, a sign of contradiction. Like an ill wind that blew the peace away. Edith's last few days in Breslau were still a recent and painful memory. 'What will you do with the Sisters in Cologne?' her mother had asked casually, thinking it was a new teaching post. Then the truth came out: 'Live with them.'[2] Peace was shattered, drowned out now by an uproar. Edith was going, deserting them. (How could she explain that it was for them, her people whom she loved so much, that she was going into Carmel?) She had embraced, said one relative, 'the religion of our persecutors'.[3]

Edith was much loved. She knew it, and she saw the full extent of the hurt she was causing. She saw her mother, despairing, breaking down. Edith was close to it herself. She had only to give in and stay, and everyone would be happy again. But Someone stronger was calling her to leave, and brought them all to the day of departure. As the first vespers

of the feast of Teresa of Avila were about to begin, Edith –
in deep peace – stepped through the Carmel door. 14 October
1933.

At last she was in the place she had longed for. This gave
her great joy. Other people, voices of the world, exclaimed at
this life of 'sacrifice':[4] leaving all to live in an austere
convent. Sacrifice? Edith was almost embarrassed. Having
been lonely in the world, shut out of Carmel, she now had
everything she wanted. Sacrifice? Yet in many ways they were
right, these voices of the world.

Carmel is a world of absolutes. God is the goal, but what
is the path to him? To quote John the Baptist's timeless words
of truth: 'He must increase, but I must decrease' (John 3:30).
It sounds wonderful, ideal ... but to human nature, there is
actually nothing more painful. To seek the all, Edith had to
become nothing, to deny herself in every conceivable way.

Denying herself in physical things: the day beginning at
half past four in the morning; the unheated, spartan cell in
which she had to kneel to use the wash jug; asking to borrow
'our pen' every time she needed to write something; abruptly
laying it down again the moment the bell rang for chapel.

Denying her mind and her will: obeying every order in a
spirit of submission; handing over her freedom to the will of
her superiors; she no longer belonged to herself ...

Only a balanced person could survive. Only a person called
by God could flourish in this environment, this voluntary
prison, and be happy.

Yet Edith was radiantly happy. She was, at long last, inside
the Carmel of Cologne. Why Cologne? Through an acquain-
tance. Yes, but providence had a large hand in it too. It was the
right place for Edith. The oldest Carmel in Germany, it had
been founded in 1637 by Spanish nuns imbued with the spirit of
Teresa. Three hundred years later, the convent had a special
apostolate of making the Carmelite charism better known – for
when Edith entered, there was a growing interest in Carmel.[5]
Normally, this work would fall to the friars, but there were no
Carmelite friars in Cologne. The nuns themselves had to stand
in, as it were. They hosted meetings of Teresian spirituality.

Moreover, some of the sisters were writers, actively using their talents to promote the riches of Carmel.[6]

Edith had given up everything to enter Carmel. Even her writing, she assumed. But as if in response to her generosity, she found that it was given back to her: as an order! In her nine years at Cologne and Echt, she was able to: complete her autobiography, *Life in a Jewish Family*; bring out the remainder of her translation of Thomas Aquinas; write her philosophical masterpiece, *Finite and Eternal Being*; produce numerous essays, plays and booklets on Carmelite history and figures, crowning them all with her study of John of the Cross which she was editing on the day she was deported: *The Science of the Cross*.

Yet Edith kept her priorities in place. It was not writing that made her most fulfilled, it was no particular activity or 'thing'. Her first duty was to pray, to seek union with God. In the world, she had astonished laypeople and religious alike by her capacity for prayer: hours spent on her knees, motionless, bright-eyed, all of which pointed to total absorption in God. Now, even in Carmel – the very house of prayer – she was still noticeable. Prayer occupied her every spare moment: she would kneel close to the tabernacle, often with arms outstretched, cruciform. Prayer gave her all her strength, kept her able to love her sisters when resentment could have been all too easy.

Edith was forty-two when she entered Carmel, about twenty years older than the novices. But maturity brought its own hardships. A natural teacher, she had nonetheless to become a 'learner'. A child, struggling to learn the rules. She had been eminent in the world. And she appeared to be making no errors in Carmel, to be walking 'the way of perfection'. All the more reason, then, why the superiors felt it their duty to humiliate her.[7] How else, it was thought, could one train someone in humility, that queen of all virtues? They did not have to look far: every day, Edith's manual work placed opportunities before their eyes.

Edith was hopeless, despite her eagerness to help. At sewing time, her needle was fast and furious, but the lopsided stitches had to be unpicked and redone. And, 'Never,' said Mother Renata, herself a graduate of domestic science, 'was there anyone so left-handed in a kitchen.'[8]

In the world, these may seem light matters and evoke an affectionate smile. In Carmel, however, even small things can be channelled into cosmic proportions. One day, Mother Renata delivered Edith a stinging reprimand: 'I have been told that in the world you were such a clever person. Here, you become more stupid every day.'[9] The sisters present saw Edith's face grow red. They watched with bated breath which, as on similar painful occasions, turned into admiration as she humbly accepted the criticism.[10] They could see the battle going on in Edith and she managed, only just, to win through.

These 'pinpricks', as Thérèse of Lisieux would call them, were all grist to the mill of the 'Little Way', the doctrine of the French saint that inspired Edith's own daily life. To quote from Edith's description:

all the little sacrifices that a regimen structured day after day in all its details demands of an active spirit; all the self-control that living in close proximity with different kinds of people continually requires and that is achieved with a loving smile; letting no opportunity go by for serving others in love.[11]

Never one to exaggerate or complain, Edith had no qualms, however, about calling the daily sacrifices 'a silent, life-long martyrdom'.[12]

The Carmelite life is 'prayer and sacrifice'. Edith thrived on the daily two hours of silent prayer. She said she realized what she had been missing before she entered Carmel.[13] Perhaps a surprising statement, given the hours she had already been used to spending in prayer. But two hours at set times were a gradual building-up of foundations, something very different from snatching an hour here and there in-between the pressures of life. 'No human eye can see what God does in the soul during hours of inner prayer. It is grace upon grace.'[14]

If Edith blossomed on prayer in Carmel, the same can be said of sacrifice. She was remarkably used to mortification already – her own carefully constructed regime! – work to excess and not much food or sleep. She now, however, had to do simply what the *Rule* demanded, and surprisingly life became a bit easier! No longer in charge of her life, Edith became relaxed for the first time. The years vanished from her face and she took on the beauty of childlike joy. And she laughed. She laughed with the other sisters, said Mother Renata, 'till the tears ran down her cheeks. She used to declare that she had never laughed so much in all her life as during recreation in Carmel.'[15] Edith laughed, sang, threw herself into her new life. But her sense of mission, of carrying the Cross, was always close to her heart.

After just one month in Carmel, Edith was asked to write something for the feast of John of the Cross (at that time 24 November). The result was the essay, *Love of the Cross*[16] – a provocative title. There is a battle, wrote Edith, sounding the war cry. Not that she mentioned specifically here the Nazi persecution of the Jews. For she looked deeper still: to the essence, the truth of what was happening in the world. The battle, she announced, was between Christ and the Antichrist, and the Cross is our weapon. The Cross will take sin and suffering out of the world; we must walk the way of the Cross.

This insistence on suffering can sound extremely grim. So can the recurrence of the word, 'Cross'; her pages are filled with it like a field that has become a war cemetery. So we need first to think what 'Cross' really conjured up for Edith, what it felt like for her, the reactions it caused in her. For this, we must go back to the source of her attraction to the Cross: to Anne Reinach, the young widow, strong and radiant. In short, a person not crushed by suffering but carried: *blessed* by the Cross.

In this essay, the words, 'joy' and 'joyous', occur almost as often as 'Cross'. How can this be? It was so because, as Edith knew, 'love of the Cross' was not love of a torture, love of a piece of wood, but love of the Person who was on the Cross. Suffering was the very place, therefore, where Edith could always find him, come closest to him, and help him to save the world.

Edith was inspired, too, by the 'mystical body'. For her, it was a key term but never an abstract concept. In fact, it was more like a three-dimensional picture. We think back to her revelation of 6 April 1933. The Cross had been laid on the Jews, she said. Those who knew it should offer to carry it. We can try to visualize what Edith saw: thousands of people staggering under the weight of a giant cross-beam.

In the essay, she returns to that graphical image. The whole of humanity is helping Christ to carry the Cross. Now, if we look more closely, the group is thinning out, people are falling away. Starting with the chosen people themselves. Followed by many of Christ's own disciples. Who are left, struggling to hold up the heavy beams? Only 'the lovers of the Cross'. They are, we have seen, the lovers of Christ. Joined to him, they too can effect redemption. But 'they' are really a 'we'. We are all called to this, writes Edith, who herself would live out her words in a uniquely intense way. That time would come.

The essay is signed, 'Dr. Edith Stein', still her name as a postulant. It was soon to be replaced by her chosen name in religion: Teresa Benedicta of the Cross. Known as Sr Bene-dicta – the name taken out of gratitude to Beuron[17] – she was flanked by two symbolic titles: Teresa, representing her conversion and call to prayer; and the Cross, which Edith would carry in Carmel and beyond. Benedicta a Cruce. It means, of course, 'Blessed by the Cross'.

15 April 1934. The clothing ceremony, and a big public event. On this day, Edith received her new name, the Carmelite habit, and the visit of numerous friends and colleagues. Hatti was there, Husserl sent a telegram, and the chapel had rarely been so full. Not one seat was occupied by a member of the Stein family; but Rosa, at least, was there with her in spirit: the elder sister who would soon become a Catholic herself.

Tucked away in the crowd was Maria Pohl, a young local woman, who hoped to be accepted by the Carmel. As the enclosure door opened to receive the new novice, Maria, the future Sr Baptista, peered into the cloister and caught a glimpse of Edith's eyes framed by the white veil. They were clear and peaceful: a gaze of total surrender. Maria longed to be there, to live alongside this inspiring Carmelite.

Edith had entered like a child wanting to run before she could walk. Knowing she was called to the Cross, she was impatient to feel the blows![18] They soon emerged, and were crushing. The daily humiliations have already been mentioned. Home and family, too, continued to be an open wound. Edith wrote to her mother every Friday but received no reply for two years. One day there arrived a greeting in her mother's handwriting; it was Edith's greatest consolation.

The Carmel itself brought Edith a bitter disappointment. The Cologne community was actually building a monastery in Breslau itself; at her interview, it had been agreed that Edith would be transferred there at the earliest opportunity. She would see her family again. But now she was not going. Of the five nuns who were selected, Sr Elisabeth objected that if a Jewish family was seen visiting the Carmel, suspicions would be raised and the convent would come to the attention of the Nazis. It was too risky.[19] And so it was decided: Edith would have to stay in Cologne. She watched them getting ready to leave and accepted, with resignation.

In the meantime, Edith continued to write, during the little time that was available. The lunchtime relaxation period was given to her for this purpose. She sat in her cell, facing out over the cloister to the novitiate through her wide-open window. In that room opposite, the other four novices were taking recreation. Sometimes they looked out of the window and caught sight of Edith poring over her work. Then they would clap so as to catch her attention. There followed friendly waves: to show her 'that she belonged to us,'[20] said Sr Baptista, who had not the slightest idea what Edith was writing. Edith would smile and wave back, before bending her head again over her page.

The smile of Edith Stein: a smile not devoid of seriousness. That is '*the* picture of her that stays with me,' wrote Sr Baptista after Edith's death.[21]

Edith had no illusions that the Carmel would guarantee her safety. She followed outside events closely, often through visits from anxious Jewish friends. Many sisters, Edith noted, disliked being called to the parlour, jerked out of their life of prayer. Edith, however, during her long wait to enter Carmel, had come to see that contemplation plunges one into the world:

> But gradually I realized . . . that, even in the contemplative life, one may not sever the connection with the world. I even believe that the deeper one is drawn into God, the more one must 'go out of oneself'; that is, one must go to the world in order to carry the divine life into it. [22]

Edith would go into the parlour hoping to bring consolation, then return to the chapel where she would lay the person's distress before the tabernacle. Over it hung an enormous painting, a life-sized picture of Christ Crucified.

In those days, before disaster struck, Edith was gradually being transformed. The Mass was not only her greatest support, it gave her Christ himself, forming her, making her identify with the very heart of her call:

> [The Saviour] lays his hand on us when we come to him, naturally most strongly when we participate in the Mass in the way required by the meaning of this sacrifice, that is, when we do not just attend and see and hear, but *sacrifice* ourselves with him, surrendering ourselves totally so as to be transformed with him and offered up with him. [23]

Shaped by the Mass every day, Edith began to find that the daily hardships were no longer so difficult. They became more spontaneous, more joyous, even a natural reflex. [24] Her call to sacrifice, to surrender, gave her that special 'eye' that saw in the word of God the message for her. It would enable her one day to give up everything, not just possessions but life itself:

> A new year at the hand of the Lord – we do not know whether we shall experience the end of this year. But if we

drink from the fount of the Saviour each day, then each day
will lead us deeper into eternal life and prepare us to throw
off the burdens of this life easily and cheerfully at some
time when the call of the Lord sounds.[25]

These words would herald the arrival of 1941. But for now,
it is still 1935. 21 April, Easter Sunday morning. A private
ceremony was taking place. The six o'clock sun peeped into
the chapel and lit up, centre stage, Edith making her first
vows to the Prioress. Afterwards, Sr Baptista saw Edith
walking in the garden with Mother Renata. Doubling back,
she caught up with them under a fruit tree. 'How do you feel?'
she blurted out. Edith, radiant, replied: 'Like the bride of the
Lamb.'[26] The 'Lamb that was slaughtered' (Rev. 5:12). Five
years later, she would encourage other sisters in their vows by
saying: 'All who want to be married to the Lamb must allow
themselves to be fastened to the cross with him.'[27]

Vows were renewed every year on 14 September, feast of
the Triumph of the Cross. It was that date in 1936. Edith had
had a difficult summer, with news from home dominated by
the illness of her mother. Edith's turn came to renew her
vows. At that very instant, she had the vivid sensation that her
mother was standing right beside her. Auguste Stein, she
learned later, had died at precisely that time. Later, Edith
would declare that her mother was interceding for her in
heaven.[28]

By 1938, the atmosphere in Germany had become extremely
dangerous. Edith became known to the authorities in April of
that year. Hitler had organized an election for the citizens to
show support for or against his recent annexation of Austria.
The voting slip contained a large circle in which to register a
'yes', and a significantly smaller one for a 'no'. All were
obliged to vote – all, that is, except for Jews who were forbidden to do so. Three officials arrived at the convent to hand out
voting slips. They counted the number, ticked off the names,
and asked why a 'Dr Edith Stein' had not yet voted. Mother
Renata gave the reason. One of the men turned to a colleague:
'Write in here that she is non-Aryan,' he said.[29]

Edith now knew that she must leave Cologne. She was putting the community at risk by her mere presence. Yet, always more clear-sighted than others, she perceived the dangers and the convent still did not. Mother Renata, now the Prioress, would not think of transferring her. Still the months went by.

In October, five years to the day since Edith entered Carmel, she was called into the parlour: it was her brother, Arno, come to say goodbye on his way to America. Meanwhile Erna, her closest sister, was also arranging to emigrate. Still nothing happened for Edith. Not until the terrible pogrom of 9 November: the *Kristallnacht* or 'Night of Broken Glass'. Throughout Germany, Jewish properties were attacked and looted, synagogues burned to the ground, Jews arrested. These state-organized riots went on until morning, when the full extent of the havoc was seen. One of the Cologne suburbs singled out was Lindenthal, the district of the Carmel.[30]

There was no doubt now: Edith had to be moved. Her first choice, Bethlehem Carmel, was not possible for immigration reasons.[31] Instead, she was welcomed to Echt in the Netherlands, a convent founded from Cologne.

New Year's Eve was her last and best chance. The following day, all Jewish passports would have to be stamped with a large identifying 'J'. Two friends of the Carmelites offered to drive Edith over the border: a priest, Leo Sudbrack, along with Paul Strerath, a country doctor. They left in the afternoon after her last-minute travel papers arrived.

Edith had grown extremely fond of the sisters, especially her superiors. She was choking back her tears during the hasty departure. At Edith's request, a small stop was made in the heart of Cologne, at the Carmelite church. This was the site of the original convent from which in 1802, during persecution of the Church by Napoleon, the sisters had been driven out.[32] Edith crept into the former nuns' choir and came as close as possible to the statue of 'Our Lady, Queen of Peace'. There, she asked for her blessing: a blessing of peace which she would take with her into the inevitable war.

Notes

1   Drügemöller, p. 7.
2   SEL, p. 26.
3   *Ibid.*, p. 108.
4   S-P, Letter 192, p. 197.
5   Edith attributes this interest to the worrying situation in Germany which in turn led to renewed recourse to prayer (HL, p. 29). She also identifies the recent canonization (1925) of Thérèse of Lisieux as another factor bringing Carmel to the attention of the public (HL, p. 1).
6   Fermín, *Edith Stein: Modelo*, pp. 176–81.
7   Pohl, pp. 99–100.
8   Posselt, p. 137.
9   Pohl, p. 75.
10   *Ibid.*, p. 99.
11   HL, p. 6.
12   *Ibid.*, p. 6.
13   S-P, Letter 168, p. 171.
14   HL, p. 6.
15   Posselt, p. 141.
16   HL, pp. 91–3. Although the editors' introduction dates the essay 'around 1934 after her entrance into the Carmel of Cologne' (p. xx), the signature, 'Dr. Edith Stein', suggests that it was written before April 1934 when she received her name in religion – that is, for 24 November 1933.
17   S-P, Letter 178, p. 182.
18   *Ibid.*, Letter 192, p. 197.
19   Batzdorff, pp. 84–5.
20   Pohl, p. 85.
21   *Ibid.*, p. 98.
22   S-P, Letter 45, p. 54.
23   ESGA 16, p. 55.
24   W, p. 121.
25   HL, p. 115.
26   Pohl, p. 91.
27   HL, p. 99.
28   S-P, Letter 227, p. 238.
29   Posselt, p. 183.
30   Anthony Read and David Fisher, *Kristallnacht: Unleashing the Holocaust*, London, Michael Joseph, 1989, p. 99.

31   In addition, Edith would have been the only Jewess in a
     community of Arab sisters – and at a time when Arab-Jewish
     tensions in Palestine were high. Possibly for this reason, there
     is no trace of an application for Edith's transfer having been
     made: *see* Neyer (ed.), p. 99.

32   Fermín, *Edith Stein: Modelo*, pp. 176–7, n. 186.

CHAPTER FOUR

THE ULTIMATE SACRIFICE

Gratitude was inscribed in Edith's nature. She was, said a confidant, 'ever thankful for the grace of conversion'.[1] And at her departure from Cologne, Edith was taken aback when one of the older sisters wept and thanked her for having been there. 'How can you say that?' Edith exclaimed. 'It is I who must thank God for having allowed me to live with you.'[2] Edith had waited twelve long years to enter Carmel and her gratitude was immense to the convent which had accepted her: a Jewess, aged forty-two, with no dowry. She was no less grateful to the community of Echt who were now offering her a home.

In that small Dutch village, seventeen nuns were waiting in anticipation. The doorbell rang, and at the enclosure door Edith was greeted by the Prioress, Mother Ottilia, and her deputy. This second person, Mother Antonia, was slightly nervous. But her fears were dispelled on glimpsing Edith: joyous, youthful ... 'not a Jewish type at all'[3] were the words that rushed into her mind. This was the face of Catholic anti-Semitism: deeply ingrained in the culture, even in charitable individuals. Antonia's shocking judgement was meant as a compliment!

Edith was given a warm welcome. Possibly there was an immediate bond, in that all but three of the nuns were German; this was the language still spoken when Edith arrived.[4] There was another reason to feel at home: the fact that Echt had been founded by sisters from Cologne. After persecution of the Church in Germany (this time by Bismarck), the Cologne Carmelites had fled, in 1875, to the Netherlands. Echt was just over the border. Those founding nuns now lay buried in the convent cemetery; on her first full day, Edith was taken to visit the graves. It was New Year's Day, 1939.

Again, Edith had much to learn. Yet there was a world of difference from her life in Cologne. Just as an apprentice learns a trade, then becomes a master, so Edith had been formed in Cologne by caring but uncompromising superiors. She was now fully trained, fully professed, and for all her youthful appearance, a mature person of forty-seven. She would launch herself into Carmelite life even more intensely than before: as a trusted member of the Order, and as a living example of her vocation to prayer and also sacrifice. For Edith, this would become the *ultimate* sacrifice.

A sign of Edith's maturity in the Order was that she was given teaching roles, one of them being novice mistress for the lay sisters. Little provision had been made for this group, but as far as Edith was concerned, choir and lay sisters should be treated the same. In this respect, she was far in advance of her time. She obtained information from other Orders on guidelines for lay sisters; she wanted them to feel, as much as possible, part of the convent family. When one of them expressed the desire to say the breviary – a practice reserved at that time for choir sisters – Edith encouraged her, at least as a private exercise; the Prioress still had to give her permission. It was refused and the breviary confiscated. And how did Edith react? She stayed silent – outwardly obedient, but inwardly disappointed and in profound disagreement. Edith had a marked sensitivity towards lay sisters, no doubt dating from the time she had got to know them so well at St Magdalena's convent in Speyer.

As with the Speyer Dominicans, so Edith again found herself teaching Latin to novices. Here, at Echt, it was as if her whole 'teacher' personality had been restored to her. The Carmelite 'pupils' found her 'patient' and 'maternal' – unless they had not

bothered to do their work, in which case she was 'pitiless'![5]
Sometimes, a local student, Anthony Mertens, would come to
the parlour to talk to Edith. She lent him the works of Teresa of
Avila, one book after the other. But each time, there was a test!
Unless he could show that he understood what he had just read,
he was not getting the next book! One day, Anthony told Edith
he was so concerned about world events that he could hardly
concentrate on his work. Edith was adamant: he should get on
with his thesis and be grateful he had the chance. Was she
encouraging him to rate his studies more highly than the war?
Hardly, since she had interrupted her own, in 1914, to train as
a Red Cross nurse. No, it seems she was telling him something
else, a message embedded in Carmelite values: to do God's will
at the present moment, to carry out our daily tasks as well as we
possibly can – to walk the 'Little Way', instead of musing on
'great' actions to which we have not been called.

   Although by now a Carmelite for five years, Edith was still
no better at practical work! The nuns at Echt looked on in
amazement at Edith trying to sweep a corridor. It was not the
normal posture of a person holding a broom. To them, it
looked like someone taking a dog for a walk: dragging the
handle while the bristly head trotted along behind her. Eventually, one side of the corridor was swept. Then Edith would
turn round and 'sweep' the same side all over again! Her
sewing was still disastrous but now had – for Edith, at least –
a more welcome result: she was no longer asked to unpick it.
Little did she know that another sister, groaning in dismay,
was being asked to redo it for her!

   How, in general, did Edith come across to the community?
In the account of one sister who is surely speaking for many
others: Edith was 'one of us'; yet there was *something* radiating from her: 'simplicity' and, yes, 'sublimity' too.[6] It was
very clear to everyone that Edith was a person of deep and
continual prayer. Like Thérèse of Lisieux, she seemed never
to lose her calm. During air raids, for example, while many
sisters were shaking in fear, Edith was noticeably motionless:
sitting in prayer, arms outstretched. A living crucifix. But she
never tried to *sound* holy. She avoided the topic of her prayer

and said nothing about her inner life. Instead, she spoke of things that would amuse: such as the Jesuits of Cologne who doctored a statue of John of the Cross until it became St Ignatius! Even the prayer time in chapel had a funny side. In the early mornings, Edith would often fall asleep while sitting on the floor, resting on her heels. Other sisters would awaken her with a nudge; she would then smile at them and go back to sleep. Edith, in her turn, was quite assiduous at giving nudges and prods!

Reminiscing years later, the sisters recalled Edith's abiding feature: that most powerful of phrases, 'radical in loving'.[7] She showed 'heartfelt sympathy, attentiveness to each person, readiness to help wherever and however possible'.[8] And she was always ready to forgive. One day, a sister said something hurtful to Edith; then, thinking better of it, ran after her. But somehow, the apology just wouldn't come out. A timid 'Sr Benedicta . . . ' hovered uncertainly on the air. At which, 'she turned round and embraced me.'[9]

By Easter, Edith felt fully at home. She wrote to Mother Petra in Dorsten: 'My basic attitude since I've been here is one of gratitude – grateful that I may be here and that the house is as it is.' But she continued: 'At the same time I always have a lively awareness that we do not have a lasting city here.'[10] Edith would have liked to settle. Still officially a member of the Cologne Carmel, she was applying to stay at Echt. But deep down, she had an intimation that she would be leaving Echt one day. And not to return to Cologne.

The 'lasting city' started to recede on Passion Sunday, 1939: the way of the Cross had begun. On that day, 26 March, Edith sent a request to the Prioress. This was her formal self-offering:

> Dear Mother: please, will [Your Reverence] allow me to offer myself to the heart of Jesus as a sacrifice of atonement for true peace, that the dominion of the Antichrist may collapse, if possible, without a new world war, and that a new order may be established? I would like [my request] granted this very day because it is the twelfth hour.[11]

The 'twelfth hour' – so urgent that it was almost too late; so pressing that nothing else would do than this signing of her own death warrant. The next day was a Monday, the usual routine of prayer and work. The same daily life – yet nothing was the same again.

On 9 June, Edith wrote her will. Books and manuscripts were bequeathed; she had nothing else to give away. Until the last paragraph, when we find that Edith has something immense to give away: her whole life. Quoted here in full, this passage is a sequel to her self-offering:

> Already now I joyfully accept the death which God has destined for me in complete submission to his most holy Will. I ask the Lord to accept my life and death for his honour and glorification, for all the concerns of the Sacred Heart of Jesus and Mary and of the Holy Church, especially for the maintenance, sanctification and perfection of our holy Order, particularly the Cologne and Echt Carmels, in atonement for the unbelief of the Jewish people and so that the Lord may be received by his own and his kingdom may come in glory, for the salvation of Germany and world peace, finally for my family members, living and dead, and for all whom God has given me: that not one of them may be lost.[12]

'Joyfully': the sign of a genuine sacrifice. Edith is accepting the death which she feels God has already destined for her. That original offering was no passing ardour, like a flame that would flicker and die when faced with reality. No: months later, Edith was no less generous in giving herself. But for what, or for whom – since the words of these offerings are not the same?

The request made in March was concise: 'true peace' – which meant doing battle against the Antichrist. A universal aim, like the massive outline of a tree. In the will of June, we now see its separate branches: all the people, places, institutions affected by that battle. Edith wishes to live and die for the Church, for the concerns of Jesus and Mary, for the Order of Carmel. Then, there are the peoples to which she belongs: the communities of Cologne and Echt, the Jews and Germans, her family, friends and acquaintances. She is offering herself for all of these.

But we must not pass by in silence that provocative phrase, 'atonement for the unbelief of the Jewish people'. On the surface, it has a terrible ring about it, suggesting condemnation of the Jews. So what does Edith really mean?

'Unbelief' does not denote lack of *faith* (as with lukewarmness), but lack of *belief* (in Christ) – just as when Edith, an agnostic Jewess, first encountered the Cross of Christ: 'my unbelief was shattered'.[13] St Paul speaks of Israel's 'unbelief' in Romans 11, explaining it by the mystery of salvation: 'a hardening has come upon part of Israel, until the full number of the Gentiles has come in. And so all Israel will be saved' (Rom. 11:25–26). Edith is surely echoing this context when she adds the words, 'and so that . . . his kingdom may come' – her offering for the Jews is a prayer for the second coming, not the need to avert condemnation. Her own mother did not accept Christ. And had not Edith declared that she was interceding for her in heaven?[14]

Three years to the day after her mother's death: 14 September 1939, again the renewal of vows. Asked to write something for the ceremony, Edith produced *Elevation of the Cross*.[15] In this essay, each sister is led in spirit to the foot of the Cross: 'The Crucified One looks down on us . . . ' It is a probing gaze – 'Will you remain faithful to the Crucified?' Why this question exactly? Because, as Edith shows, the Cross represents the vows – taken to their radical conclusion. Jesus, she writes, went to the Cross out of *obedience* to his Father; hung there destitute through choosing *poverty*; and 'spilled his heart's blood to win your heart': an invitation to *purity*. 'The arms of the Crucified are spread out to draw you to his heart. He wants your life in order to give you his.'

'He wants your life.' Edith renewed her vows as if taking them for the first time – as a commitment for life, a commitment to *give* life, or even give *up* life. Every Carmelite was called to *give* life: 'bound to him by the faithful observance of your holy vows, your *being* is precious blood . . . poured everywhere – soothing, healing, saving.' And giving *up* life? Any sister who saw the occasion as no more than an annual ritual would have been struck by the intensity which Edith injected into it. 'If you decide for Christ, it could cost you your life.' But were they not in the safe, 'neutral' Netherlands?

Edith's immediate concerns, that summer of 1939, were mostly with Germany. Erna and her family were at least safe in New York now. Their brother Paul, however, was still in Breslau, as was Frieda. Rosa was another worry. Having become a Catholic on Christmas Eve 1936, when staying with Edith in Cologne, she was now housekeeper for a woman in Belgium who intended setting up a convent. This person, however, proved an impostor, and Rosa was made a virtual slave. A contact of the Carmel had gone to rescue her.

Edith was telling this to the Provincial, Cornelius Leunissen, at the beginning of July. He was sympathetic and offered to do anything he could to help. After he left, Rosa caused a huge surprise by turning up on the doorstep, penniless but safe. Echt Carmel now became her home – though Rosa was not, as she had hoped, an extern sister (a role with no precedent at Echt) but a tertiary living in the convent.

With Rosa, Edith had someone who understood the real evils of the Nazi regime. It grieved Edith that the nuns had very little idea of what Hitler was like – but then, they had not been living in Germany. Sometimes, Edith even heard anti-Jewish remarks in the convent. She would reply that the Jesuits, too, were wrongly maligned.[16] As with Mother Antonia's initial impressions of Edith, it was not a question of malice but of ingrained prejudice. In fact, the sisters had much affection for Edith, even because of her Jewish background.

They knew how much Edith nourished herself on the Old Testament. So, if we look ahead to her fiftieth birthday in 1941, we will see the sisters giving her a 'Jewish' treat: a play, written by themselves, featuring patriarchs and prophets. But how would they identify the characters? 'Moses' came on stage, the incongruous figure of a petite little nun wearing a large nose. Edith burst out laughing. She knew it was all meant in good part and they wanted to please her. But still, it was like indulging 'the Jewish sister', someone who was different. It was a far cry from being able really to understand.

If Edith was conscious of being isolated, she also saw it as a privilege. She said one day to a priest: 'You don't know what it means to me when I come into the chapel in the morning and, seeing the tabernacle and the picture of Mary, say to myself: they were of our blood.'[17] Rosa would know, of course, and so would Ruth Kantorowicz, another close Jewish contact at this time. A friend from childhood and a rather anxious personality, Ruth had also converted and entered Carmel, in Maastricht; she was rejected ten months later. She was now living as a home help with the Ursulines at nearby Venlo, where she spent much time typing up Edith's manuscripts.

The Netherlands were invaded by the Nazis on 10 May 1940. Suddenly, the place of refuge was gone. Edith and Rosa had to present themselves to the Gestapo and the SS. They had to fill out numerous forms, giving their personal details and whereabouts. The offices of the Gestapo were in Maastricht, a good twenty miles from Echt and a time-consuming journey. One day in November, the helpful Fr Cornelius decided to save Edith and Rosa the trouble and go there for them. He was accused of 'favouring Jews' and roughly turned away. After he left, the Gestapo issued a warrant for his arrest. Fortunately, he was tipped off and escaped just in time. By now, the convent began to realize the dangers.

The sisters noticed that Edith was continually sad. It was all the more poignant as she tried to hide it with a smile. Other things were obvious, too. Any early risers were likely to glimpse, through the wide-open window of Edith's cell, a figure kneeling in prayer with her arms outstretched. 'In the Carmel of Echt,' writes one source, 'it was an open secret that Edith Stein had for long been quietly training herself for life in a concentration camp, by enduring cold and hunger.'[18]

They suspected she might be sent to some sort of camp, but no one thought it would mean death.

Not wanting to burden the sisters with her worries, Edith must have been relieved to get to know the local priests. Two frequent visitors were Jan Nota and Johannes Hirschmann, Jesuits from nearby Valkenburg, who became close friends of hers. Nota was a philosopher, with an understanding of phenomenology; Edith confided to Hirschmann some of her most heartfelt concerns.

Hirschmann soon saw that when Edith spoke of her 'people', she meant not only the Jews but the Germans. In a sense, her love went out to both the oppressed and the oppressors. 'Who,' she kept asking herself, 'will atone for what is happening to the Jewish people in the name of the people of Germany?'[19] She was horrified to know that baptized Christians, such as Hitler and Himmler, were taking such guilt on themselves. One day, she exclaimed to Hirschmann: 'Who will turn this enormous guilt into a blessing for both peoples?'[20] He was struck by the answer she gave to her own question: the victims of that hatred. It was therefore the victims, willingly carrying their sufferings, who could atone.

These are crucial statements. They take us right back to Edith's self-offering in March 1939, as 'a sacrifice of atonement'. And they take us back even further: to Edith's birth, in 1891, on the Day of Atonement. She grew up knowing that this day, *Yom Kippur*, was her special feast. In an essay written before her conversion, she had drawn a sharp distinction between 'atonement' and 'punishment'. Punishment, she wrote, is imposed, whereas atonement is voluntary.[21] Before ever she entered Carmel, therefore, she understood the meaning of atonement. It now took on a vital resonance for her.

The Day of Atonement is described in Leviticus 16. Once a year, the high priest would enter the Holy of Holies in the Temple of Jerusalem. Animals were offered up for the sins of both the priest and the people. Two of these sacrificial animals were goats: one of them (the 'scapegoat') was burdened with the people's sins and sent into the wilderness; the other was slaughtered and its blood shed on the ark of the covenant. Both of these goats, wrote Edith, symbolize Christ: an outcast, he bore our sins; and his blood was shed for us. 'The Day of Atonement is the Old Testament antecedent of Good Friday.'[22] So, too, the high priest prefigures Jesus. But atonement does not stop there. We, too, continue to carry the Cross of Jesus but 'by no means deny that Good Friday is past and that the work of salvation has been accomplished. Only those who are saved, only children of grace, can in fact be bearers of Christ's cross.'[23]

What, though, is atonement? It is quite literally 'reconciliation' – both in German (*Versöhnung*) and in English (at-one-ment). It is reconciliation between people and God. They are like two banks of a river, and only a bridge in-between can reconcile them. Jesus is that bridge, drawing all people to the Father. Edith saw the Carmelite vocation as just such a bridge: 'it is our vocation to stand before God for all.'[24] Think again of the river banks. The bridge belongs to those two banks: it has a foot in each of them. That is why it has special importance when Edith speaks of 'her people': she belonged to them and she belonged to Christ, she was a bridge between them even when one of the banks was the Nazis, Hitler or Himmler. And all the people mentioned in her will: the Jews and Germans, family and friends, Carmel and the Church, indeed the whole world. She belonged to these spheres and stood before God for all.

But atonement is not only a prayer of intercession, it involves sacrifice – hence the Carmelite charism of prayer *and* sacrifice. Among the Temple sacrifices which Edith knew so well from the Old Testament, atonement involved the ultimate sacrifice. There were basically three kinds of offerings to God: a sample, like the first fruits; a portion, like the communion sacrifice divided among the people, priests and God; finally, there was a sacrifice in which everything was given to God. This was the 'holocaust'.

Already in 1930, when Edith was impatient to lead the life of a Carmelite, she wrote of the necessity of her own '*holocaustum*';[25] she used the Latin form of the word as it appeared in the breviary. Thérèse of Lisieux also chose this term (in its French form) when she offered herself to God's Merciful Love as a *'victime d'holocauste'*. What is the meaning of the word? It comes from two Greek words: *'holos'*, meaning 'whole', and *'kaustos'*, meaning 'burnt'.

The holocaust in the Temple was therefore completely burnt – which is why it was completely offered up to God. There is another aspect of this type of sacrifice, too: the smoke that rose in the air. The Hebrew word for 'holocaust' – *'ôlâ* – means 'that which ascends'. For Edith, a born Carmelite and with knowledge of Hebrew, this would surely resonate with her very being, for the Carmelite path is indeed the *'ascent* of Mount Carmel'.

A new year arrived. 1942 was like an intensified version of 1933, both of them fateful for the Jewish people and for Edith. In January 1933, Hitler had come to power, and shortly afterwards Edith had received her vocation to carry the Cross for the persecuted Jews. Now, in 1942, those two events grew to their dreadful climax. In January, Hitler held the infamous 'Wannsee Conference' in Berlin, which approved the 'Final Solution': the annihilation of all the European Jews. This would set in motion Edith's own death: the fulfilment of that earlier call to carry the Cross.

It was the fourth centenary of the birth of John of the Cross. For this Carmelite anniversary, Mother Antonia, now Prioress, asked Edith to write a book on the saint. She may have thought it would take Edith's mind off the worrying situation outside. In fact, it did the opposite. For even as it absorbed Edith, it was constantly focusing her mind on the Cross. Gradually, she was preparing herself for arrest. There was an affinity with the Spanish saint removed from his convent and imprisoned in Toledo: 'To be helplessly delivered to the malice of bitter enemies, tormented in body and soul, cut off from all human consolation and also from the strengthening sources of ecclesial-sacramental life – can there be a harder school of the cross?'[26] This work, *The Science of the Cross*, is a rewriting of John's night symbolism into the language of the Passion. The active night of the senses becomes the *via dolorosa* – when we actively carry our Cross. In the passive night, we are crucified. With stark realism, Edith pointed out that we cannot crucify ourselves; it *has* to be passive. We need other people to put us on the Cross.

Those others were the Nazis, set to exterminate the Jews, and the Swiss authorities, unable to take many more refugees.[27] Edith and Rosa had been accepted by two Swiss Carmels, Le Pâquier and Seedorf, but were still awaiting permission to leave. Pinned under Edith's scapular was a slip of paper with the words: 'When they persecute you in one town, flee to the next' (Matt. 10:23). Yet, incredibly, she was not worried, and she immersed herself in her writing. In this last book, she gives the Cross a threefold nature: as message, doctrine and path. This third element is the climax: to follow and embrace the Cross in the circumstances of life.

Since the Nazi invasion in 1940, persecution of the Jews had become ever more intense. First there were exclusions from the rest of society; then whole families were deported. These measures brought the Churches together, and in 1942 they decided to make a stand. In February, they met the *Reichskommissar*, Dr Seyss-Inquart. Then in mid-July, when further deportations became known, they sent a joint telegram to protest.[28]

There came an unexpected reply. In order to quieten their protest, Seyss-Inquart announced that the baptized Jews were safe. But no such exception had been asked for, and still the other Jews were being deported. The Churches therefore decided to take stronger action: to make their protest public. Seyss-Inquart heard of this and flatly forbade them. The Catholic Church, however, did not comply. And so, on Sunday 26 July, the fateful pastoral letter was read out from every Catholic pulpit in the Netherlands.[29] As it included the news that baptized Jews were safe, many people would have felt relief. If so, they could not have been more wrong. The next morning, a furious Seyss-Inquart ordered, in retaliation, that all the Catholic Jews be deported.

The following Sunday, 2 August. The SS vans had been travelling up and down the country as from dawn. With two hundred and forty-four arrests to make, it took all day. The doorbell rang at Echt Carmel at five o'clock in the evening, during prayer. Edith was called out of the chapel and ordered, with Rosa, to leave straightaway. Edith dashed back inside, knelt imploringly before the Blessed Sacrament, then whispered, 'Pray, please, sisters!' She disappeared again before most of the others knew what was happening. One sister tried to feed Rosa scrambled eggs on a spoon, as Rosa was shaking too much to hold it. Edith declined any food. She was completely calm. Then the two of them came out into the street. It was a shocked crowd outside, indignant at the arrests. One neighbour, Maria Delsing, heard Edith say to her petrified sister: 'Come, we are going for our people.' The hour had come, the hour of the ultimate sacrifice.

Late that night, they reached Amersfoort concentration camp and were thrown into barrack blocks for a sleepless night. In the morning, Edith and the others, practically all priests and nuns, divided the large room into men's and women's quarters. The women gathered together to pray the breviary and the rosary. Edith's calm, reassuring presence made her the unofficial leader of the group.

The next day was a Tuesday. It was 4 August and they were transferred to Westerbork camp – a curious-looking huddle dressed in religious habits and wearing the yellow star. We know something of Edith's companions. There was Rosa, of course, and also Ruth Kantorowicz. 'The two dear children are here,' Edith jotted down in a note she was allowed to send to Echt: she was speaking of Elfriede and Annemarie Goldschmidt, fresh-faced girls of only nineteen and twenty. Then there was Alice Reis, one of Edith's goddaughters. And the impressive Löb family with five Trappists dressed in white.

To anyone who took a closer look, Edith stood out like the quiet centre in a whirlwind. Her serenity was evident even when she was at her most active – washing and caring for children in the camp, as did many of the sisters. She did not spend her time worrying, as did others; nor, like the Löb family, did she plan all the work she would do in the future.

When there was nothing to do but wait around, Edith would just sit. Praying. Overwhelmed by sadness.

For her people, not for herself. One eyewitness, a Frau Bromberg, noted a tell-tale sign: Edith Stein, she said, was too calm to be worrying about herself personally. Edith just sat in silence. From time to time, she would look up at Rosa and smile. A smile, said the woman, so 'unspeakably sad' that it was painful to see. This same eyewitness described Edith in the memorable words: 'a Pietà without the Christ'.[30]

One other summer, 1916, Edith had visited Frankfurt on her way to the doctoral exam. Visiting a museum, she had walked up to the 'Mourning Group'. Four life-sized sculptures: Mary and John, Mary Magdalen and Nicodemus. Four figures on Calvary – without the Christ. Edith had been drawn into their mourning, in a way she had felt truly at home there, for she had hardly been able to drag herself away.

She was there now, on her own Calvary, in her own mourning group. Sitting with Rosa, cheering up Ruth. And seeing the terrible distress of her people, the Jews – the Christ – on whom the Cross was laid. She had once offered to help carry that Cross – nine years ago, on her first visit to the Carmel of Cologne, and her resolve had not wavered. Now, here at Westerbork, a Dutch official was impressed by this nun 'whom I think the Vatican may one day canonize. From the moment I met her ... I knew: here is someone truly great. For a couple of days she lived in that hellhole, walking, talking, and praying ... like a saint.'[31] He offered to help her escape. To escape death? Her reply: 'If somebody intervened at this point and took away her chance to share in the fate of her brothers and sisters, *that* would be utter annihilation. But not what was going to happen now.'[32]

Only six people, Frau Bromberg included, were left standing there early on the Friday morning. Waving goodbye, as the hundreds of people were herded onto a train. Several hours later, it came to a brief, unexpected halt at Schifferstadt. This small town was right next to Speyer. Edith peered out, called to three different people on the platform, and dropped a note onto the tracks, which a priest picked up and gave to two teachers from St Magdalena's: 'Greetings from Sister Teresia Benedicta a Cruce. *En route* for the East.'[33]

The 'East' was Auschwitz, and the 'route' ended in the early hours of Sunday morning, 9 August. Edith's first – and last – stop was the gas chambers.

A long time before – twelve years before – Edith had sensed the need for her *holocaustum*, the call to be offered up in the total and ultimate sacrifice. The *Shoah* itself should not, as it often is, be called the 'Holocaust': for that would imply that the Nazis were high priests, and the gas chambers and crematoria the Temple. But as the smoke rose up, that Sunday in 1942, it was uncannily – chillingly – the sign of a sacrificial holocaust, atoning for those responsible and, as Edith believed, turning the hatred into a blessing.

Notes

1   Posselt, p. 151.
2   *Ibid.*, p. 185.
3   Leuven, p. 128.
4   Dutch was soon adopted, not least because of the arrival of five Dutch postulants in 1941: *see* Fermín, *Edith Stein: Modelo*, pp. 207–8; Edith rapidly mastered this language.
5   Testimony of Sr Stephanie, in Herbstrith (ed.), *Never Forget*, pp. 256–7.
6   Leuven, p. 140.
7   *Ibid.*, p. 138.
8   *Ibid.*, p. 139.
9   *Ibid.*, p. 134.
10   S-P, Letter 300, p. 309; cf. 'For here we have no lasting city, but we are looking for the city that is to come' (Heb. 13:14).
11   S-P, Letter 296, p. 305 (which gives 'propitiation' in place of 'atonement').
12   Leuven, pp. 148–9.
13   Posselt, p. 59 (the meeting with the widowed Anne Reinach).
14   See S-P, Letter 227, p. 238.
15   See HL, pp. 94–6.
16   Herbstrith (ed.), *Edith Stein: Ein Lebensbild*, p. 122.
17   *Ibid.*, p. 134 (the priest was Johannes Hirschmann, SJ).
18   Neyer, *Edith Stein: A Saint*, p. 27.

19 Herbstrith, *Edith Stein: A Biography*, p. 194.
20 *Ibid.*, p. 194.
21 From her *Investigation on the State* (1920–1921; published 1925); quoted in Schandl, p. 149.
22 HL, p. 12.
23 *Ibid.*, p. 93.
24 S-P, Letter 174, p. 178.
25 *Ibid.*, Letter 52, p. 60.
26 SC, p. 29.
27 *See* the letters from the Swiss authorities, in Neyer (ed.), p. 125 and ESGA 3, Letter 763, pp. 579–80.
28 Reproduced in Prégardier and Mohr, pp. 38, 40 (date of telegram is 11 July 1942).
29 Reproduced in *ibid.*, pp. 41–2, 44–5.
30 Testimony recorded in *ibid.*, pp. 52–3.
31 Herbstrith, *Edith Stein: A Biography*, p. 186.
32 *Ibid.*, p. 187.
33 Feldes, *Edith Stein und Schifferstadt*, p. 74.

Part II

Ideal Figures in Edith's Prayer

CHAPTER FIVE

JESUS: EMPATHY IN PRAYER

The 'Other'

'Christ is the centre of my life,' announced Edith confidently.[1]
She was a recent convert and writing to her philosopher
friend, Roman Ingarden who, to her eyes, needed shaking out
of his religious apathy! She was also proclaiming the truth
about her new life: Jesus the focus of her thoughts, the core
of her whole being, that most significant 'Other' who was
even forming her into himself. And Edith had always had a
sense of the 'other'.

She was the author of a thesis on empathy. A subject she
had chosen herself – but not as a mere academic exercise. She
had a genuine desire to understand people, and we should take
her at her word when she wrote, in another letter to Ingarden,
'My works are only ever expressions of what has preoccupied
me in life'.[2] In life, Edith was truly empathic – a person of
inner silence who put herself in others' shoes. Family, friends
and students confided their most intimate troubles to her. So
did at least one husband and wife as they moved towards
divorce.[3] If she won the confidence of each of the parties, it
is because they recognized in her an objective, unbiased
friend. There is no place in empathy for prejudice or a hidden
agenda. It is at the heart of empathy to listen and be receptive.

We should not handle God any differently. In prayer, Edith listened to God in the same way that she gave her rapt attention to a person in need: 'The only essential is that one finds, first of all, a quiet corner in which one can communicate with God as though there were nothing else'.[4] Even when still an agnostic, she seemed to suspect that empathy was as relevant to God as to people. Hence her astonishing statement at that time, that empathy is how believers understand God and God understands people.[5] After her conversion, whole realms of understanding opened up for her, because through Jesus she had access to understanding God, revealed in his humanity. 'Whoever has seen me has seen the Father' (John 14:9). St Paul had gone before her, that great man of empathy: 'we have the mind of Christ' (1 Cor. 2:16). Edith, who had spent half her life seeking to understand people, now sought to know the mind of Christ.

'Formed' into Christ

To know the mind of Christ. This sounds sublime – but is it? Think of what Edith says about true community, in this case the lack of it:

> If one diplomat has fathomed what the other is thinking and hence infers what step he himself has to undertake,... the starting point for his inference is the state of affairs 'that the other *is thinking* this.' No common thinking gets underway.[6]

So, for Edith, it is never enough just to *know* what the other is thinking, as a piece of useful information. An expert in theory, she was also a woman of action who applied her knowledge to real life. It is useless to know the mind of Christ if it has no impact on our lives. Edith wanted to know Christ so as to become like him. To be 'another Christ' – that, she said when lecturing to educators in Munich, is the goal of religious education.[7]

She began to give the matter some thought: how to go about making oneself like Jesus. And before long, the truth hit her

between the eyes: it is impossible! But no need to despair:
God himself will do the work of transformation. So how does
God do it? That was her next question.

Edith now developed her key notion of 'forming'.[8]
'Forming' a person, she would say, goes deeper than 'teaching' facts or 'educating' (leading) towards a particular goal.
Sculpture is her favourite image in this connection: 'that
highest art, of which the material is not wood or stone but
living human souls.'[9] God, for Edith Stein, is the Divine
Sculptor:

> The eternal Artist, who creates material for himself
> And forms it into images in various ways:
> By gentle finger strokes and also by chisel blows.
> But he does not work on dead material;
> His greatest creative joy in fact is
> That under his hand the image stirs,
> That life pours forth to meet him.[10]

Yes, to be formed by Christ involves 'meeting' him. And in
her writings, Edith gives us three privileged places in which
we encounter the living Christ: the Eucharist, the Gospels,
silent prayer. She gives us her method, she gives us her
insights – into the mind of Jesus.

The Eucharist

Had she not been Teresa Benedicta 'of the Cross', Edith could
well have been 'of the Eucharist'. She had a whole spirituality in this area, which she called the 'three Eucharistic
truths':[11] Jesus is present in the tabernacle, offered up in the
Mass, joined to us in communion. This place, *par excellence*,
of the Real Presence is where forming is especially strong.

To onlookers, Edith was always by the tabernacle. Pupils,
colleagues, retreatants looked on in astonishment – and
maybe a sense of inadequacy – at the young woman kneeling motionless for hours on end. But what does this tell us
about Edith – other than her enviably sturdy knees? That she
was fully absorbed in Jesus, certainly. More helpful than rear

views, though, are the ones face to face: Edith assuring Sr
Reingard that she was not tired after spending the whole night
in prayer ('Tired – with him!'); or the Ursuline sister who
saw Edith's sparkling eyes.[12] Here before the tabernacle, says
Edith, the mysteries of faith become clear, the darkness of
our path is illumined as if by lightning. Jesus forms our
understanding.[13]

The meaning of the Mass itself, she continues, is sacrifice.
And if we sacrifice ourselves with him, Jesus 'lays his hand
on us'.[14] To understand the real depths of these words, we
must look beyond the image of the sculptor's hand. For with
her Jewish upbringing, Edith knew that the priests in the
Jerusalem Temple laid their hands upon the victim for slaughter (cf. Lev. 8:14). This is a forming with potentially fatal
consequences.

Finally, communion. A few words suffice to say everything: it is 'completion of union ... There is no stronger reli-
giously forming influence.'[15]

Empathy with Jesus in the Eucharist
What are Edith's insights, that she can share with us, into the
mind of Jesus?

First, though, a proviso. There is no single mind of Jesus.
Like the colours of a rainbow, every insight, though valid, is
only part of the spectrum. The suffering servant of Mark's
Gospel is a far cry from the Jesus of John. For Francis of
Assisi, Jesus was a pauper, for Dominic a preacher, for
Teresa a person of prayer. It all depends on their own calling
– on *our* own special calling. We could say we have been
given a unique pair of eyes to spot that colour in the rainbow
which everyone else has missed.

So what did Edith perceive in the Jesus of the Eucharist?
It was not, as it is with some, Christ ministering to the
hungry.[16] Edith saw only 'the Lamb that was slain'.[17] In the
Irish town of Knock, Jesus appeared as a lamb on the altar.
Edith had never been to Knock. But her Jesus was indeed the
Passover lamb on the altar. And she knew that to know
means to follow: at her first vows, she called herself 'the

bride of the Lamb';[18] after final profession, she offered up
her life.

Perhaps, though, her finest insight is into the Jesus who
'first loved us' (1 John 4:19). He takes the initiative; in
modern jargon, he is pro-active! The 'three Eucharistic truths'
may encourage *us* to visit the tabernacle, attend Mass and
receive communion. But rather, they are about *Jesus* looking
at us, sacrificing us with himself, coming to us in union.
Edith's is a perspective of empathy: the Eucharist from Jesus'
point of view. When she prayed before the tabernacle, she was
not staring at a metal box: she was being looked at in return.
No wonder the Ursuline sister did not find her yawning! And
thus, Edith perceived the mind of Jesus as a longing to bridge
a gap, to exchange his residence on the altar for the temple of
the human heart. The Eucharistic truths take us into that gaze
of longing that streams out from the tabernacle:

> That, O Lord, is your royal throne on earth,
> Which you have erected, visibly, for us,
> And it gives you pleasure to see me coming up to it.

> You lower your gaze full of love
> Into my eyes,
> And you lean your ear
> Towards my whispered words,
> And you fill with peace
> The depths of my heart.

> But your love is not satisfied
> With this exchange
> In which still we are left divided.
> Your heart is longing for more.

> You come to me each morning, as my early meal.
> Your flesh and blood become my food and drink
> And something wonderful takes place.

Your body, mysteriously,
Penetrates mine,
And your soul
Unites itself with mine:
I am no more
What once I was.[19]

In the Eucharist, Edith sees the sacrificial victim who longs to transform us, to 'penetrate' us with himself. Receiving communion is becoming one flesh with Christ – one flesh and one mind.

The Gospels
'Hear, O Israel: The Lord is our God, the Lord alone' (Deut. 6:4). Throughout the ages, God's command to us has been to 'listen' to the Scriptures – to scan them with a listening heart and thus come to know God. 'Let anyone with ears listen!' (Matt. 13:43). The Gospels themselves are an inexhaustible source for knowing Jesus. 'I am constantly discovering in them new lights,' wrote Thérèse of Lisieux;[20] and Edith likewise: 'We can never finish studying the Gospels.'[21]

It was the Gospels that gave Edith an understanding of her vocation in Carmel. Like almost all Carmelites, she saw the heart of the *Rule* as 'meditating on the Law of the Lord day and night and watching in prayer'.[22] This is not literally a call to spend one's life studying the 'Law' – that is, the Torah – but to contemplate the embodiment of the Law, Jesus: 'We thus fulfil our Rule when we hold the image of the Lord continually before our eyes in order to make ourselves like him.'[23]

But there seems to be a problem here: the words, 'in order to make ourselves like him'. Has not Edith already said that we *cannot* make ourselves like him – that only God can transform us? This perennial question, the conflict between active and passive behaviour, is well stated by David Torkington:

To follow Him, doesn't mean that we should try and copy Him as an artist copies a model. It doesn't mean that we should merely imitate the outward manifestation of the inner light that burned in Him. It means that we must expose ourselves to that self-same light that it may set us afire too.[24]

Note the word, 'merely'. Imitation of Jesus *is* necessary; but it only really becomes possible after we have been touched by grace. Edith found herself explaining this point when she was once misunderstood. In November 1930, she spoke on the nature of woman's soul: it should be expansive, quiet, warm and so on. Following this lecture, intrigued members of the audience contacted Edith, asking for advice on how to acquire all these qualities. So she wrote an article, published just over a year later, to clarify her meaning:

> I believe that it is not a matter of a multiplicity of attributes which we can tackle and acquire individually; it is rather a single total condition of the soul, a condition which is envisaged here in these attributes from various aspects. We are not able to attain this condition by willing it, it must be effected through grace.[25]

Therefore Edith, striving to become 'another Christ', *first* opened her heart to the Gospels to understand the mind of Jesus. And she received the deepest insights. But to put them into practice was a matter of grace. In a striking echo of her poem on the Eucharist quoted above, Edith says that if we take the image of Jesus into ourselves, we are 'penetrated' by it[26] – the same term for the action of the host at communion. Then, Edith tells us, the words and deeds of Christ become 'a living power' within us.[27] Why? Because, to quote one authority on *lectio divina*: 'This is not simply an encounter with a piece of writing, even though divine. It is an encounter with the living God.'[28]

Empathy with Jesus in the Gospels
An encounter with the living God, yes – but who is the God Edith met? What was it about Jesus that leapt off the page for

her? Which images came back to her time and time again? For there *were* such constants for Edith as she contemplated the life of Jesus from the crib to the Cross.

He did the Father's will. This so impressed Edith that several times in her works she quotes these words from Gethsemane: 'Your will be done!' 'This,' she says, 'was the content of the Saviour's life'; and these words should be our own 'guiding stars'.[29] Edith sees in Jesus a man 'who not only promptly obeyed his heavenly Father, but also subjected himself to people who imposed the Father's will on him.'[30] Writing here for Carmelites on the vow of obedience, she straightaway perceives this double surrender by Jesus – no doubt because of her own equivalent situation of obeying superiors who represented the will of God for her. Reading the Gospels, then, is a two-way movement, as Edith's case shows: she isolates qualities in Jesus from the Gospels; and she does so, too, because she is already sensitized to them from her own experiences. If 'Your will be done!' were inspirational words for her, it was in all likelihood because in 1941 when this talk on the vows was written, Edith was faced, like Jesus, with the threat of danger.

On other horizons in her life, these same words were 'guiding stars' for Edith. Ten years earlier, when about to resign her teaching post but unable to enter Carmel, they meant abandoning herself – her whole future and security – into the hands of God. A procedure that seemed to her so obvious that she was quite scathing about those Christians who are given to worrying:

> To be a child of God means to go hand-in-hand with God, to do his will, not one's own; to place all our hopes and cares in his hands and no longer be concerned about one's self or future. Thereupon rest the freedom and the good cheer of the child of God. Yet how few of the truly devout, or even those truly heroic and willing to make sacrifices, possess them ... They are all familiar with the parable of the birds in the sky and lilies of the field. But whenever they encounter anyone who has no means, nor income, nor

insurance, and is none the less unconcerned about the
future, then they shake their head, completely baffled.[31]

This passage, from *The Mystery of Christmas*, comes under
the section entitled, 'Thy will be done!' Edith learned from
the words and example of Jesus that surrendering our will to
God's is the only way to be free.

Edith's pupils at Speyer had not realized she was Jewish
until one day, in a literature lesson, she taught them the legend
of Ahasuerus, *The Eternal Jew*: this figure, said to have
refused Jesus a rest against his house wall on the way to the
crucifixion, was condemned to wander restlessly throughout
the world until the Second Coming. Migration is a *leitmotif* of
the people of Israel, beginning with Abraham: 'strangers and
foreigners on the earth' (Heb. 11:13); the flight to Egypt;
wandering in the desert; arrival in the promised land, only to
be exiled again throughout the course of history. Jesus is a
typical example of this fate. Edith writes of him, concerning
the Carmelites' vow of poverty:

> His birth in a stable, his flight to Egypt, already indicated
> that the Son of Man was to have no place to lay his head.
> Whoever follows him must know that we have no lasting
> dwelling here ... Today it is good to reflect on the fact
> that poverty also includes the readiness to leave our beloved
> monastery itself.[32]

This is Christ's poverty for Edith, not in a basic sense of
going without, but in a modern-historical context: one feels
that Edith is showing Jesus as typifying the fate of the Jewish
people in her own times. She had already quoted these very
words from Hebrews (13:14) – 'we do not have a lasting city
here'[33] – as she faced up to the possibility of leaving the Echt
Carmel to flee the Nazis a second time. Her situation allows
her to empathize with Jesus in his own plight on earth and,
without doubt, to feel that he was empathizing with her too.

Most of all, Jesus is love. That is, of course, cast-iron
doctrine, accepted by every believer. Edith is sensitive in

particular to Jesus' relationship of love with the Father – which, as we shall see, also includes his life of prayer. Keeping the perspective of eternity, Edith was surely nourished by John's Gospel, especially its Prologue (and also, no doubt, by the *Romances* of John of the Cross):

> The eternal Father in unconditional love has given his entire being to his Son. And just as unconditionally does the Son give himself back to the Father. The passage of the God-Man through temporal life could alter nothing of this complete surrender of Person to Person. He belongs to the Father from eternity to eternity and could not give himself away to any human being. He could only incorporate the persons who wanted to give themselves to him into the unity of his Incarnate Divine Person as members of his Mystical Body and in this way bring them to the Father.[34]

Here, we find revealed the heartbeat of Edith Stein, joyfully allowing herself to be absorbed into this relationship. In Edith's view, nothing distracts Jesus from the Father, nothing causes him to turn away even for a split second. He is always turned towards the Father. We could perhaps think of the image of the magnet, which the French language so aptly calls '*aimant*' – 'loving'.

Yet, for Edith, the loving Jesus is treading the boundary of sadness. Sad, like the 'little shepherd' of John of the Cross, because his love is not returned. This can even happen with consecrated souls, and it seems to Edith that Jesus on the Cross is pleading with them for their love: 'Will you remain faithful to the Crucified? ... He has spilled his heart's blood to win your heart.'[35] This is a most moving and human statement. Every person with a smattering of theology knows that Jesus died of love – to save our souls. But, in Edith's eyes, he died of love – to win our hearts.

Silent Prayer
Edith Stein was a woman of prayer. She was especially called to silent prayer, solitary dialogue with God. This is what led

her to Carmel. It led her also to a new and exciting way of knowing God. In 1941, after eight years in Carmel, Edith wrote *Ways to Know God*; the very title shows that her quest was unabated.

Silent prayer, like the Eucharist and the Gospels, is a privileged place of encounter with God. We might even say that this prayer goes further than the Gospels, insofar as the latter consist of images and words. That, Edith writes in *Ways to Know God*, is because 'it is still more important to be touched by God inwardly without word and image.'[36] This inner touch, she tells us, is nothing less than 'personal experiential knowledge of God'.[37] It is vitally important for knowing God:

> For in this personal encounter the person comes to know God intimately, and this knowledge enables him for the first time to 'shape the image according to the original.' ... He alone can recognize *his* God, the God whom he knows personally, in the 'portraits'.[38]

What does Edith mean, when she speaks of 'the original' and 'portraits'? It can be helpful to think of ourselves looking at photographs. If we know a man well, it goes without saying that we will recognize him in a photograph, even a slightly blurred one. But if someone shows us a picture of a stranger, then recognizing that person in the flesh is near impossible – anyone who has tried to meet a visitor at the airport will know this problem! So what Edith is saying is that if our only contact with Christ is through images, he will always, in a way, be a stranger for us. But once we have that direct, personal contact – the experience of God in the soul – the pictures will fall into place and add to our knowledge.

We have seen, in connection with the Gospels, that Edith selected certain pictures of Christ that spoke to her most strongly: surrendered will, poverty and exile, love. There is one more image, central to Edith's vision of Christ: Jesus the person of prayer. Edith's experience of prayer was so much a natural reflex that she not only noticed this aspect of Christ in the Gospels but shaped it still more, she added to it. Note her description of Jesus praying to his Father: 'Surely,' she writes, 'this dialogue was life-long and uninterrupted. Christ prayed interiorly not only when he had withdrawn from the crowd, but also when he was among people.'[39] It is Edith's own suggestion – hence her word, 'surely' – that Jesus prayed all the time he was among people. Actually, no one would dispute this view, but we just need to point out that it is not explicitly stated in the Gospels. It is the intuition of a person of prayer.

Empathy with Jesus in Prayer

Jesus at prayer in the bustle of the crowds. In this example, Edith is empathizing with Jesus, putting herself into his mind. And something else too: just a little, she is projecting her own mind and personality onto his. Really, there is nothing artificial or forced about this. It is, we may say, a question of kindred spirits. Edith, described by a Benedictine priest as 'standing in the world of time and yet apart from it',[40] looked at Jesus and saw exactly the same in him. The 'apartness' is, of course, not aloofness but constant prayer.

Notably, Edith calls the prayer of Jesus a '*secret dialogue*'.[41] There is nothing unusual about this, it is Gospel language: 'pray to your Father who is in secret' (Matt. 6:6). But it is also a word that makes us think of Edith. Both as a child, dubbed by her sisters 'a book sealed with seven seals', so reluctant was she to disclose her thoughts.[42] And many years later, struggling with spiritual conflict, unwilling to expose it beyond the confines of her heart. That is when she uttered to Hatti the words which many people have come to associate with Edith: '*Secretum meum mihi*', 'My secret is mine'.[43] Edith may also have been thinking of the meaning of this phrase in John of the Cross: 'Be silent concerning what God may have given you and recall that saying of the bride: *My secret for myself.*'[44] When Edith sees Jesus in 'secret dialogue', it is likewise an almost nuptial union, so to speak, between himself and the Father.

But it is a secret that cannot be kept. The inner dialogue of Jesus may be hidden to the crowds standing around him in

Galilee or Judea. Yet within the communion of prayer – a totally different relationship from standing next to God in the street! – Edith's experience is that converse from God to the soul is freely flowing:

> Prayer is the communication of the soul with God. God is love, and love is goodness giving itself away. It is a fullness of being that does not want to remain enclosed in itself, but rather to share itself with others.[45]

This feel for God's self-giving nature is the fruit of Edith's firsthand experience of God in prayer. It leads her to suggest – again with a 'surely' – this feature of Christ in the Gospels: overflowing; held back only by human inability to understand. On the Last Supper discourses, Edith writes:

> He knew that this was their last time together, and he wanted to give them as much as he in any way could. He had to restrain himself from saying more. But he surely knew that they could not bear any more, in fact, that they could not even grasp this little bit.[46]

This is about Jesus communicating with people. But what can we learn, from Edith, of his speaking with the Father? She begins with the Gospel – with John 17, where 'once he allowed us to look extensively and deeply at this secret dialogue.'[47] This prayer at the Last Supper, much loved by Carmelites, is known as the 'high priestly prayer': it refers back to the Day of Atonement when the high priest entered the Holy of Holies, praying for the sins of himself, his household and his people. The sacrifices of this day have been explored in the last chapter in connection with Edith's 'holocaust'. But as a person of prayer, she saw Leviticus 16 as a prayer scene also: it is, writes Edith, a 'solitary dialogue [that] took place in deepest mystery'.[48] Jesus is the new high priest, and Edith encourages everyone to read again his words in John 17: 'All who belong to him may hear how, in the Holy of Holies of his heart, he speaks to his Father; they are to experience what is going on and are to learn to speak to the Father in their own hearts.'[49]

At this point, Edith makes a transition from reading the Gospel to listening to the heart of God:

> The Saviour's high priestly prayer unveils the mystery of the inner life: the circumincession of the Divine Persons and the indwelling of God in the soul. In these mysterious depths the work of salvation was prepared and accomplished itself in concealment and silence. And so it will continue until the union of all is actually accomplished at the end of time.[50]

In one fell swoop, we have made two important moves. We no longer see Jesus sitting at table in an upper room in Jerusalem, but find him in the place where he belongs for all time: the heart of the Trinity. And we have also put down our Bibles (just for a while) and been spirited away into the presence of the three Divine Persons, like a welcome guest taking the empty seat at that other famous table, the one in Rublëv's Trinity icon.

How can this have happened? The key that, quite literally, opens everything up is 'the mystery of the inner life'. When we are at silent prayer, resting in the presence of God in the soul, we have this 'mystery of the inner life'. So, too, do the Persons of the Trinity when they converse, says Edith Stein. In putting these two relationships side by side, she is showing that there is common ground: that what takes place in the heart of God and in our own soul at prayer is of the same nature. There can be no greater tribute to silent prayer, no greater incentive to be faithful to it every day.

The gift that Edith has to offer us from her experience of prayer is the discovery of *silence*. An unshakable inner silence. The testimony of Fr Raphael Walzer – of importance as he was her spiritual director – records that 'her interior spirit remained in tranquillity, blissfully gazing and rejoicing before God.'[51] Silence is the common ground between the Divine Persons and our prayer. It is also, Edith sees, the means by which God speaks to our soul. *Depends on us* to listen to his will. Silence is the channel of communication, like a heavenly telephone:

> The decision for the Redemption was conceived in the eternal silence of the inner divine life. The power of the Holy Spirit came over the Virgin praying alone in the hidden, silent room in Nazareth and brought about the Incarnation of the Saviour . . . The Virgin, who kept every word sent from God in her heart, is the model for such attentive souls in whom Jesus' high priestly prayer comes to life again and again.[52]

How does it take place in Mary – in us? Not by our memorizing John 17 and repeating the words like a parrot. Not even by our repeating the themes of petition – prayer for the Church, for unity – that is, trying to pray in the spirit of Jesus. Rather than this, it is letting the Holy Spirit pray in us. That is the prayer of Jesus, the new high priest:

> All authentic prayer is prayer of the church. Through every sincere prayer something happens in the church, and it is the church itself that is praying therein, for it is the Holy Spirit living in the church that intercedes for every individual soul.[53]

To pray in the Holy Spirit! That is how we may, like St Paul whom we quoted at the beginning, 'have the mind of Christ'. And then, Edith exclaims: 'What could the prayer of the church be, if not great lovers giving themselves to God who is love!'[54]

Only through love can there be perfect likeness to God. This likeness is true empathy in prayer: empathy with Jesus, and a reaching out in understanding and compassion to all God's people.

Notes

1   ESGA 4, Letter 96, p. 168.
2   *Ibid.*, Letter 78, p. 143.

3   Richard and Nelli Courant (*see* LJF, pp. 374–6, 381–4); Edith was also mediator in the marriage difficulties of Max and Else Gordon (*ibid.*, pp. 99–101).

4   S-P, Letter 45, p. 54.

5   *See* PE, p. 11.

6   PPH, pp. 214–5.

7   ESGA 16, pp. 51–2.

8   *Formung*; also *Bildung* (see *ibid.*, pp. 53–62, 93).

9   *Ibid.*, p. 93.

10   HL, p. 119.

11   ESGA 16, pp. 64, 56.

12   These two accounts are in, respectively, Herrmann, p. 62 and Posselt, p. 114.

13   ESGA 16, p. 55.

14   *Ibid.*, p. 55.

15   *Ibid.*, p. 55.

16   *See*, for example, Monika K. Hellwig, *The Eucharist and the Hunger of the World*, Kansas City, Missouri, Sheed & Ward, 1992.

17   HL, p. 99.

18   Pohl, p. 91.

19   From *Ich bleibe bei euch ...* (*I will remain with you ...*), my translation: *see also Mount Carmel*, vol. 50, no. 2 (April–June 2002), p. 48.

20   *Story of A Soul: The Autobiography of Saint Thérèse of Lisieux*, tr. John Clarke, OCD, Washington, DC, ICS Publications, 1996, p. 179.

21   HL, p. 4.

22   *Ibid.*, p. 3 (referring to point 10 of the *Rule*). For different perspectives on what constitutes the focus of the *Rule*, see *Mount Carmel*, vol. 50, no. 1 (January–March 2002), pp. 8–22, 54–60.

23   HL, p. 4.

24   *The Hermit: A Personal Discovery of Prayer*, New York, Alba House, 1999, p. 50.

25   W, p. 143.

26   ESGA 16, p. 54.

27   *Ibid.*, p. 54.

28   Mariano Magrassi, OSB, *Praying the Bible: An Introduction to Lectio Divina*, Collegeville, Minnesota, The Liturgical Press, 1998, p. 31.

29 HL, pp. 103, 11.
30 *Ibid.*, p. 103.
31 MC, pp. 13–14.
32 HL, p. 102; cf. Heb. 13:14.
33 S-P, Letter 300, p. 309.
34 HL, p. 104.
35 *Ibid.*, pp. 94–5.
36 KF, p. 108.
37 *Ibid.*, p. 106.
38 *Ibid.*, pp. 108–9.
39 HL, p. 11.
40 Posselt, p. 85; the priest is Fr Damasus Zähringer.
41 HL, p. 11; my italics.
42 LJF, p. 437.
43 Herbstrith (ed.), *Edith Stein: Ein Lebensbild*, pp. 87, 95; the phrase is from the Vulgate: Isa. 24:16.
44 *The Sayings of Light and Love*, # 153, in *The Collected Works of Saint John of the Cross*, trs. Kieran Kavanaugh, OCD and Otilio Rodriguez, OCD, Washington, DC, ICS Publications, 1991, p. 96.
45 HL, p. 38.
46 *Ibid.*, p. 11.
47 *Ibid.*, p. 11.
48 *Ibid.*, p. 12.
49 *Ibid.*, p. 12.
50 *Ibid.*, p. 12.
51 Posselt, p. 151.
52 HL, pp. 12–13.
53 *Ibid.*, p. 15.
54 *Ibid.*, p. 15.

CHAPTER SIX

MARY: OUR MODEL AND MOTHER

Early every morning in the Carmel of Echt, the chapel door would open and Edith would walk in, pause for a moment before a picture of Mary and think: she and I are of the same blood. Edith never failed to find it incredible: this woman, the mother of God, her own relation! Confiding this thought one day to a Jesuit priest, she said: 'You don't know what it means to me'.[1] Maybe he didn't know. But what he could tell was just how much Mary meant to Edith.

As the years went by after her conversion, Edith found herself more and more rooted in Mary. Even her public lectures began to shine out with Mary's presence. In one of her earlier talks, in 1928, Edith spoke on the nature and vocations (or professions) of woman.[2] Two years later, she was again speaking on women's professions. This, her Salzburg lecture, made her name, and we can see why. The same themes appeared, but accompanied this time by the indelible presence of Mary, whom Edith presented to all women as their model.

That is the same as saying: Mary is a real person, to be *imitated* – not a figure on a pedestal, to be admired from a distance. How Thérèse of Lisieux longed to preach this very message and never had the chance.[3] But Edith did, and she proclaimed it firmly from the lecturer's podium:

the imitation of Mary is not *fundamentally different* from the imitation of Christ. The imitation of Mary includes the imitation of Christ because Mary is the first Christian to follow Christ, and she is the first and most perfect model of Christ.[4]

This is the language of Vatican II and after: '[The Virgin Mary] is worthy of imitation because she was the first and the most perfect of Christ's disciples.'[5] As so often, Edith was ahead of her times.

Imitation is one thing; relationship is another. This is what Edith had with Mary: 'a personal trusting association'.[6] It was so vital for her that she almost felt in despair when she saw devotion to Mary being taught through singing hymns and waving flags. That is no help to girls' lives at all, she once said at a meeting in Augsburg, pointing her words at youth leaders in the Church.[7] Edith's own gratitude to Mary was unbounded: she knew that the very thing that mattered most to her came from Mary – her Carmelite vocation: 'I thank you for having called me before I ever knew that the call came from you.'[8]

So, there are two ways of perceiving the Virgin Mary: as a model for our lives (but with the risk of seeing only the historical figure); and as intercessor and help (with the risk of prizing devotions above the lessons of the Gospel). Edith's love for Mary was whole and balanced because she embraced both perspectives: she saw Mary as both our model and our mother. Let us look now at how Mary is a model for the entire life of woman.

Model of Womanhood

'Mary is the prototype of pure womanhood,' said Edith while teaching at the institute in Münster, her very last place of employment.[9] Was she perhaps looking back on her life, at the many stages in which she had experienced 'womanhood' at first hand? She was, from birth to death, a *daughter*: the youngest child of Auguste Stein; the nun who wrote to her prioress from the concentration camp, signing herself, '[Your]

grateful child'. She was a *sister*: not just to two brothers and
four sisters but to her philosophy colleagues as well, who
appreciated her sisterly encouragement, and of course to the
Carmelite community. From Auguste Stein, she had a positive
image of the *mother* – noble, firm and affectionate – and was
herself maternal towards younger people. Edith was a *professional woman* – competent as a lecturer, teacher, even as a
nurse during the First World War. In pre-conversion days, she
sometimes imagined herself as a future *wife* (she had a good
idea who might be her future husband, too!); and she lived
this out as 'spouse of Christ', a *consecrated woman*. In her
maturity, she now knew that womanhood, in all its aspects,
needed Mary. Francis de Sales made exactly this point when
he said that God made Mary 'pass through all states of life,
so that all people may find in her whatever they need to live
well in their own state of life'.[10]

But was it enough just to be a woman – to follow nature?
Edith would shake her head. No, she would answer, quoting
the maxim, 'Grace perfects nature'.[11] Who better, then, as a
model of womanhood than she who was 'full of grace'?

To learn from Mary, Edith went back to roots: to Eve. We
could well find this surprising. After all, isn't Eve a sinner?
Sometimes, Edith put forward this view and contrasted Eve
with Mary[12] – but she did not forget that Eve was God's ideal
of woman. Edith was quite clear on this: in Eve is revealed
the nature of woman; in Mary is found that same nature,
perfected by grace.

Eve was created as a 'helpmate' to the man. *'Eser kenegdo'*
in the Hebrew, which Edith explained to her audience. It
meant, she said, a helper as if face-to-face with him[13] – but
not just a 'helpmate suitable to him', a kind of mirror image,
as some translators put it. In Edith's eyes, that would be
missing something of the original meaning – woman as a
counterpart to man: 'they complement each other as one hand
does the other.'[14] What Edith was saying was that a mirror
image is identical to the original, whereas a left and right hand
may *seem* the same – but are in fact opposites![15]

And now we get to the essence of this helpmate, this Eve,

this prototype of Mary who is herself the prototype of all women. It comes from the two names given to Eve in Genesis: as 'woman', she is a *companion*; as 'Eve', she is named a *mother*.[16] Edith therefore concluded: 'The clear and irrevocable word of Scripture declares what daily experience teaches from the beginning of the world: woman is destined to be wife and mother.'[17] There is just a chance that Edith may have winced when uttering these words, as if expecting a backlash from independent women glad to be free of the kitchen sink. Edith herself, though, was just as independent. That is why she did not mean these words literally. In fact, she was convinced that it is both possible – and necessary – for woman to be a 'wife' and 'mother', *even if* unmarried and without children. All this will become clear later.

For those women who *were* wives and mothers in the literal sense, Edith was very encouraging. In a day when it was the norm for a woman to give up work if she married, Edith once argued that married women made better teachers: they brought with them 'a big plus' to the teaching profession.[18] She was just as positive when speaking on married women in the eyes of the Church. Edith dismissed any notion of hierarchy that would make consecrated people a spiritual elite, with lay-people not quite making the grade! She saw the mother and virgin as overlapping and parallel vocations: a mother, she said, has a *spiritual* role for her children, a virgin has a *maternal* role for other people.[19] Through the figure of Mary – the *Virgo-Mater* – there is no contradiction between the two vocations.[20] Again, Edith Stein was ahead of her times. Think, for example, of *Mulieris Dignitatem*, written by John Paul II in 1988 and possibly influenced by Edith whom he beatified the previous year: '*Virginity and motherhood co-exist in [Mary]:* they do not mutually exclude each other or place limits on each other. Indeed, the person of the Mother of God helps everyone – especially women – to see how these two dimensions, these two paths in the vocation of women as persons, explain and complete each other.'[21]

This document also shows how the different vocations exist in relation to each other: '*One cannot correctly understand virginity* – a woman's consecration in virginity – *without referring to spousal love.*'[22] This is what we learn from Edith Stein too: that each vocation – wife, mother, professional or consecrated woman – sheds light on the others; what she says about one is enriching for all. And the reason is that they all have their source and model in Mary:

> Were each woman an image of the Mother of God, a *Spouse of Christ*, an apostle of the divine Heart, then would each fulfil her feminine vocation no matter what conditions she lived in and what worldly activity absorbed her life.[23]

Model of Wife and Mother
Edith was not starry-eyed about marriage, but she knew that young people often are. At one lecture in Munich, when her audience were young women teachers, the expression on their faces must have been a sight to behold. Young girls look forward to a happy family life, she told them. Well – 'I believe that even most of the "happy" marriages are, more often than not, at least *in part* a martyrdom.'[24]

Edith had listened to people in the throes of divorce, and she had a shrewd idea about where things went wrong. What struck her was that the very qualities of woman's nature were the exact places where that nature, if distorted, caused most damage. Woman, she would often say from the podium, has by nature an interest in people – this is what makes her ideally suited for marriage and motherhood. But what a danger when this very interest becomes overbearing and possessive – it no longer fosters growth but stunts it: 'The dominating will replaces joyful service. How many unhappy marriages can be attributed to this abnormality! How much alienation between mothers and growing children and even mature offspring!'[25] We can imagine that Edith had a few people in mind right at that point!

Edith would also have stressed the word, 'will' – it was always important to her. The dominating will ruins everything. This makes Mary a salutary model for women in married life: she surrendered her will; she was a 'handmaid'

– not of her husband, but of God, seeing 'marriage and motherhood as a vocation from God; it is carried out for God's sake and under His guidance.'[26] Edith advised women to look at Mary – to contemplate her. After all, she did this herself.

She looked at Mary as spouse of Joseph. And she saw a woman – quiet, trusting, silent. A woman given to 'faithful communion in suffering'[27] – which is another way of saying that she embodied 'the feminine gifts of empathy and adjustment'.[28] But it suggests something else too, and here Edith would have felt it with her whole being: Mary was able to *suffer with* – in other words, to have 'compassion'. In one stroke, we are at the foot of the Cross; but long before then, Mary was a person of compassion. Edith, too, was 'suffering with' – suffering with her people.

Then she gazed again and saw Mary as mother of Jesus:

> In the centre of her life stands her son. She awaits His birth in blissful expectation; she watches over His childhood; near or far, indeed, wherever He wishes, she follows Him on His way; she holds the crucified body in her arms; she carries out the will of the departed. But not as *her* action does she do all this: she is in this the Handmaid of the Lord; she fulfils that to which God has called her. And that is why she does not consider the child as her own property: she has welcomed Him from God's hands; she lays Him back into God's hands by dedicating Him in the Temple and by being with Him at the crucifixion.[29]

Edith saw here the ideal mother but also the disciple of Christ: Mary, that first and most perfect disciple, did Jesus' will and placed him at the centre of her life. Edith also noted how Jesus was given back to the Father – she was possibly giving a hint of corrective to those women possessive of their children. But Edith was not hard. On the contrary, she could sense the trauma when the *centre* of one's life disappears. It struck her in another way in Frankfurt years earlier, when looking at the 'Mourning Group': four figures on Calvary facing towards a poignantly empty space. Even when she thought of the mother independently of Mary, there was always the echo of the pain of the mother of God: '[The woman] has the gift thereby to live in an intimately bound physical compass and to collect her forces in silence; on the other hand, she is created to endure pain'.[30] This quiet, uncomplaining pain is Edith's vision of the Pietà: 'The pain of the Mother of God is as great as the ocean; she is immersed in it. But it is a totally restrained pain'.[31] The mother, too, she saw as a mediator: between her husband and the children, her husband and God;[32] the image of Mary, 'our advocate', was surely informing her vision. But it was mostly as spouse of Joseph and Mother of Sorrows that Mary, for Edith, was the perfect model of wife and mother.

Model of Professional Woman
At Ludwigshafen in 1928, Edith stood up to speak on woman and national life. She began by recalling the two extremist positions of twenty years earlier. The traditionalists: woman's place is in the home. And, in reaction, the extreme left: women are just the same as men. Edith found both views abhorrent. Yet, by borrowing from each, she formed a middle way between the two. No, she said, women are not the same as men, but they should not stay at home either; rather, they should be a *wife and mother in the workplace.*

There was another reason why she linked the wife and mother to the professions. It hurt her to see so much frustration among women (indeed, men too). These were the people who had a job instead of a vocation. She said, on another occasion: 'Whoever regards his work as a mere source of income or as a pastime will perform it differently from the person who feels that his *profession* is an authentic vocation.'[33] She did not show her own frustration, but it was there nonetheless. In her present post at Münster. And especially during the Speyer experience: there, she had been drawn irresistibly towards the religious life, towards vocation; there, she had also been run into the ground by endless school work – a job, a mere 'duty'.[34] This gave her heartfelt compassion for any woman whose sense of vocation, whether to marriage or the cloister, was thwarted by circumstances: 'In both instances, the danger exists that she views her life as a failure, that her soul becomes stunted and embittered, that it does not provide the strength for her to function fruitfully as a woman.'[35] Edith therefore showed her audiences how a woman *can* 'function fruitfully as a woman' in the midst of the world, even in an uncongenial environment.

It was a lesson that she first had to learn herself. Being a 'support' to others was being a *companion*; helping them develop was the role of a *mother*.[36] This is how she envisaged the idea of a wife and mother in the workplace. Some professions, she said, lent themselves more easily to the feminine nature: teaching, social work, medicine. She often thought of her sister Erna, a gynaecologist, whose plaque and bell hung on the outside wall of the Stein family home – Erna: quiet, kind and skilled. But politics needed women too, said Edith, who just after the War had joined the German Democratic Party. She knew what experience had always shown her: that women's feel for concrete situations would make them a vital counterbalance to men's leaning towards the abstraction of laws.[37] What, though, of the more masculine jobs, such as factory work? Edith could not see even that as an obstacle to the fulfilment of the feminine nature:

> woman's intrinsic value can work in every place and thereby institute grace, completely independent of the profession which she practises ... Everywhere the need exists for maternal sympathy and help,... *motherliness* ...; in accordance with the model of the Mother of Mercy, it must have its root in universal divine love for all who are there, belaboured and burdened.[38]

We can almost visualize a buzz in the audience: eyes lighting up at the thought that their mundane jobs were not what they seemed. For Edith was proposing an apostolate of charity, in imitation of the Mother of Mercy. And of Mary in her most efficient and considerate guise: 'Mary at the wedding of Cana in her quiet, observing look surveys everything and discovers what is lacking. Before anything is noticed, even before

embarrassment sets in, she has procured already the remedy
... Let her be the prototype of woman in professional life.'[39]

Model of Consecrated Woman

Edith's own calling. How every word she says emerges from
her own aspirations, resonates with her very being. Her
lectures are like an autobiography in abridged, third-person
form. But it is easy to read 'Edith' between the lines. She is
at once the speaker and an avid listener.

Edith turned to the Virgin Mary and contemplated her as
virgin. The audiences were not allowed to misunderstand
Mary: she was not a virgin merely because of the timing of
the Annunciation; no, she made a positive choice before *and
after* the birth of Christ and thus gave us a precedent for
seeing virginity as a vocation in its own right.[40] The Virgin
Mary was also the spouse of Christ, wrote Edith in a later
essay: 'there was woven between the soul of the divine Child
and the soul of the Virgin Mother the bond of the most intimate unity, which we call betrothal.'[41] Edith showed that
there is no contradiction between Mary's being both spouse
and mother of Christ: for Mary is the new Eve.

Edith saw Mary, as model for the spouse of Christ, standing 'beside' Jesus, like Eve 'by the side' of Adam.[42] She used
this phrase again and again to show how Mary was Christ's
complement and shared his qualities: 'In her virginity, she is
the pure prototype of womanhood because she stands beside
Him who is the prototype of all manhood';[43] she is 'co-
redeemer by the side of the Redeemer'.[44] When Edith looked
at Mary as mother, she saw her taking on the role of Eve as
'mother of all living creatures'. This, for Edith, was surely
the most striking example of grace perfecting nature: '[Mary]
is the mother of the living not because all succeeding generations come from her but because her maternal love embraces
the whole Mystical Body with Jesus Christ its head.'[45] A
maternity not of nature but of grace.

We can imagine the sparkle in Edith's eyes as she spoke on
the consecrated woman as 'spouse of Christ'. This role, she
said in the closing moments of a lecture in Aachen, 'is the

most sublime vocation which has been given'.[46] Her inspiration for this was the life of Mary, a side-by-side companionship on earth: 'the Saviour and his mother wandered the streets of Judea and Galilee';[47] and especially after the Resurrection: 'The Risen One is always with you! I really believe that he has never left you.'[48] And closing her lecture at Salzburg, she described the path of women, who share the divine life, in just those terms: 'we walk by the side of the Saviour'.[49]

We can easily think that Edith's lectures were on 'woman' alone. This is not true. For 'woman' is seen with her full significance only in relation to 'man'; Edith was always comparing the two. That, no doubt, is why she gained the interest of both men and women in her audiences. Speaking on religious life, she decided to discuss the consecrated man. Does he stand by Jesus' side? Does the priest imitate Mary? No, was her answer, the priest is 'a proxy of Christ', 'the type of "another Christ"'.[50] Edith believed everyone was called to be 'another Christ', but in Mary, she came to see that woman lives it in a different way: another Christ but in the feminine form. That was why she imitated Mary, knowing this was simultaneously the imitation of Christ.

Suddenly, did Edith see the men in the audience sitting bolt upright? 'Women's ordination' would have greeted their ears. Fearlessly, Edith stated that there was no dogma against it. But she believed that women were not meant to be priests: woman, she felt, has – by nature – a fundamental position at the side of Christ. Not an inferior position, but a privileged one: 'the Lord will never allow His consecrated bride to stray from His side'.[51] With these words, she closed the question; but she opened up the beauty of the role of consecrated woman – a role as spouse, yes, but also as spiritual mother.

Who can forget Thérèse of Lisieux when she heard that a great criminal, facing execution, refused to repent? How she prayed for him, 'employed every means imaginable', looked out for the newspaper and read that, at the last moment, Pranzini had kissed the crucifix three times: 'my *first child*,' said Thérèse.[52] Spiritual maternity is the work of redemption, the work of engendering souls for the kingdom. Edith would soon be giving her whole life for this purpose, exchanging the podium for the work of carrying the Cross. This is the role of the consecrated woman, of Mary, and even of God himself. Edith was sensitive to the Holy Spirit, that Person of the Godhead whom she saw as typically feminine, spreading goodness throughout the world. And the Holy Spirit came to rest in the soul of the Virgin Mary:

> we find [the Holy Spirit] again in woman's destiny as 'Mother of the Living'. The Spirit goes out of itself and enters into the creature as the begetting and perfecting fruitfulness of God ... The pure image of feminine nature stands before our eyes in the *Immaculata*, the Virgin. She was the perfect temple, in which the Holy Spirit took up his dwelling and deposited as his gift the fullness of grace.[53]

A true contemplative, Edith was attuned to the indwelling of God in the soul. She gazed on Mary as 'perfect temple' of the Holy Spirit, and saw in her the perfect model of the Church.

Model of the Church
Edith was addressing a youth group in Augsburg. She was going to talk to them about their role as women in the Church. But it seemed to her that they needed to have the whole picture before them. Of how a woman *is* the Church:

> The original cell of all redeemed humanity is Mary ... Before the Son of Man was born of the Virgin, the Son of God conceived of this very virgin as one full of grace, and He created the Church in and with her.[54]

This is the 'Immaculate Conception': redeemed humanity, the beginning of the Church. And 'the Church stands by the side of Christ like an independent person.'[55] This person is the *new Eve*. Edith explained: 'by that is meant Mary, but, at the same time, also the whole Church'.[56]

The listeners at Augsburg were privileged participants!

Sitting there, on a July day, they were privy to Edith's most intimate ideas on the Church. The new Eve, she said, is not just *by* the side but *from* the side: 'The creation of Eve from the rib of the first Adam becomes a prefigurement for the emergence of the new Eve ... from the opened side of the new Adam.'[57] Edith was now evoking the new Adam on the Cross, blood and water flowing *from* his side, the Mother of God standing *by* the side but also, as the Church, born *from* the side. And how were they side by side? As head and heart:

> [Mary] is also a unique organ of the Church, that organ from which the entire Mystical Body, even the Head itself, was formed. She might be called, and happily so, the heart of the Church in order to indicate her central and vital position in it.[58]

This, too, is our role. We know this already from Thérèse of Lisieux, and Edith was perhaps thinking of her famous phrase: Love in the heart of the Church. That Eureka experience – Thérèse discovering her true vocation within Carmel, within the Church: as its heart, the heart that burns with love and enables the rest of the Church to function.[59]

Once, Edith addressed these words to Mary herself: 'you are now always present because you are the heart of the Church.'[60] What Edith meant was the *praying* heart of the Church, the model of the Church at prayer. Exactly those thoughts came to mind when she tried to visualize Pentecost: the emerging Church gathered around that silent woman, whose prayer helped to draw down the Holy Spirit on them all.[61] Just like the Holy Spirit, the praying heart of the Church is the most effective agent for renewal:

> In the silent dialogue with their Lord of souls consecrated to God, the events of church history are prepared that, visible far and wide, renew the face of the earth. The Virgin, who kept every word sent from God in her heart, is the model for such attentive souls in whom Jesus' high priestly prayer comes to life again and again. And women

who, like her, were totally self-forgetful because they were steeped in the life and suffering of Christ, were the Lord's preferred choice as instruments to accomplish great things in the church: a St. Bridget, a Catherine of Siena.[62]

This is prophetic language! As from 1 October 1999, there are three women patron saints of Europe: Bridget of Sweden, Catherine of Siena and ... Edith Stein. In spirit, and now in truth, Edith belongs to that group, with Mary their 'model'.

A model and a mother. Remember that Edith both imitated Mary and entrusted herself to her. She longed to pass on this experience to all women:

> Those women who wish to fulfil their feminine vocations in one of several ways will most surely succeed in their goals if they not only keep the ideal of the *Virgo-Mater* before their eyes and strive to form themselves according to her image but if they also entrust themselves to her guidance and place themelves completely under her care. She herself can form in her own image those who belong to her.[63]

Edith's voice may have lingered on the word, 'if' – a big 'if': if we do not entrust ourselves to Mary, she cannot fully function as our mother.[64] A model is one thing: we can admire it, imitate it, be inspired by it. But we have no *relationship* with a model: only with a *mother*.

Mother of the Church, Mother of us all

In April 1938 Edith, now Sr Benedicta, was on retreat, preparing for final vows. The timing was perfect for a Carmelite named, 'of the Cross': it covered Holy Week and the Triduum, the whole of the Paschal Mystery. Alone and in silence, Edith turned to Mary as her companion.

During this retreat, Edith kept a diary.[65] It was not intended for publication, and so gives us a privileged glimpse into Edith's heart; to read it feels like eavesdropping. There may be a gulf of difference between the diary of Edith Stein with its fair share of theological reflections, and the personal note-

book of St Bernadette, simple and uneducated. But it is hard
to find any difference at all between Edith's intimacy with
Mary, and that of the visionary of Lourdes: 'O my beloved
Mother,' writes Edith;[66] and Bernadette: 'O Mary, my tender
Mother.'[67] Sometimes, Edith calls Mary 'Queen' – writing at
the 'Queen of Peace' Carmel of Cologne – but for Edith, as
for Thérèse of Lisieux, Mary was 'more Mother than
Queen'.[68]

Mother in a special way: as mother of Carmel. Even more
so as mother of the Church:

> When Jesus saw his mother and the disciple whom he loved
> standing beside her, he said to his mother, 'Woman, here
> is your son.' Then he said to the disciple, 'Here is your
> mother.' (John 19:26–27)

This is no bland statement; these are words of power, words
that make something happen: 'Like when he said, "This is my
body," Jesus made the bread his body, and when he said,
"Behold, your mother" and "Behold, your son," Jesus made
Mary John's mother and John Mary's son. He didn't just
proclaim Mary's new maternity, he instituted it.'[69] Edith, too,
saw something vital *happen* at the Cross: 'Mary *became* our
mother beneath the Cross. She loves the souls who follow the
Lord right up to beneath the Cross.'[70] This was the core of
Edith's own vocation: to carry the Cross with Jesus, to stand
with Mary on Calvary, to labour for the Church. At the Cross,
that very place where the Church was instituted.

There, 'woman' became 'mother' (cf. John 19:26–27).
These words are loaded with meaning. 'Woman' designates
the mission of Eve – to prefigure the new Eve of salvation
history. Edith's diary begins at this point, recalling the proto-
gospel (Gen. 3:15).[71] The term, 'mother', is equally significant: mother of all the living, mother of Jesus, mother of the
entire Mystical Body – 'Beneath the Cross she has received
the inheritance of her Son, as mother of the redeemed [she]
has taken everyone into her heart.'[72]

Like mother, like daughter. The inheritance is ours as well.

It passes through the generations of the Church, and lands at
the feet of those who are called to labour for souls, to carry
the Cross. In the last chapter, we met Edith's expression,
'laying his hand': it was the hand of Jesus the Divine Sculptor, or the priest who takes hold of the sacrificial victim. In
the diary, it appears again, now addressed to Mary – as a bond
of possession, the call to be absorbed into Christ: 'He has laid
His hand on you, [and] taken your life completely into His
own. Just so has He laid His hand on me, and you have laid
your hand on me, so that I may carry the Cross with you
both'.[73]

Good Friday, 15 April. The only diary entry that day was
a poem. It sums up the themes which Edith had been ponder-
ing during the previous days, indeed years: Mary at the Cross,
mother of the Church, her mission to work for the salvation
of every soul. But it is about us too: we also have received
souls as a bequest, and we have that same mission to stand,
for them, at the foot of the Cross with Jesus. Standing *by* his
side, engendering souls *from* his side – with our eyes turned
to Mary, our model and mother.

JUXTA CRUCEM TECUM STARE

Today I stood with you beneath the cross
And felt distinctly, more than I ever did before,
That you, beneath the cross, became our mother.
How the devotedness of just an earthly mother
Is anxious to carry out her son's last wish.
But you were the handmaid of the Lord –
Your being and life were totally surrendered
To the Being and Life of the incarnate God.

So you have taken his own into your heart
And with the heartblood of your bitter pains
Have purchased life that's new for every soul.
You know us all: our wounds, our weaknesses.
You also know the radiance of heaven;
Your Son's love wants to pour it

All around us, in eternal clarity.
Thus you guide our steps with care,
No price for you too high to lead us to the goal.

But those whom you have chosen as companions,
Surrounding you one day at the eternal throne,
They here must stand, with you, beneath the cross
And purchase, with their heartblood's bitter pains
The radiance of heaven for the priceless souls
Whom God's own Son bequeaths to them, His heirs.[74]

Notes

1   Herbstrith (ed.), *Edith Stein: Ein Lebensbild*, p. 134; the priest is Johannes Hirschmann.
2   *The Significance of Woman's Intrinsic Value in National Life*, in W, pp. 253–65.
3   *St. Thérèse of Lisieux: Her Last Conversations*, tr. John Clarke, OCD, Washington, DC, ICS Publications, 1977, pp. 161–2.
4   W, p. 201.
5   *Marialis Cultus*, # 35.
6   W, p. 201.
7   *Ibid.*, p. 248.
8   GK, p. 91; Edith also asserted that all vocations come from Mary: *see* HL, p. 105.
9   W, p. 201.
10 Eunan McDonnell, SDB, *God Desires You: St Francis de Sales on Living the Gospel*, Dublin, Columba Press, 2001, p. 134.
11 'Grace perfects nature – it does not destroy it.', quoted in W, p. 51.
12 *See*, for example, *ibid.*, p. 119.
13 *Ibid.*, p. 61: 'a helper as if vis-à-vis to him'.
14 *Ibid.*, p. 61.
15 The Hebrew expression also has an adversarial meaning, a 'helper over and against him': *see* Jonathan Sacks, *Radical Then, Radical Now: The Legacy of the World's Oldest Religion*, London, HarperCollins, 2000, p. 79.
16 W, pp. 61–2, 64.
17 *Ibid.*, p. 45.
18 ESGA 13, p. 52.

19   *Ibid.*, pp. 53-4.
20   W, p. 241.
21   *Mulieris Dignitatem*, # 17; *see also* # 19 and 21.
22   *Ibid.*, # 20.
23   W, p. 54.
24   ESGA 13, p. 50.
25   W, p. 47.
26   *Ibid.*, p. 48.
27   *Ibid.*, pp. 47-8.
28   *Ibid.*, p. 115.
29   *Ibid.*, p. 47.
30   *Ibid.*, p. 100.
31   S-P, Letter 199, p. 204.
32   W, p. 260.
33   *Ibid.*, p. 44.
34   Herrmann, p. 73.
35   W, p. 124.
36   *Ibid.*, p. 256.
37   *Ibid.*, pp. 263-4.
38   *Ibid.*, p. 264.
39   *Ibid.*, p. 51.
40   *Ibid.*, pp. 198-9.
41   HL, p. 98.
42   W, p. 200.
43   *Ibid.*, p. 200.
44   *Ibid.*, p. 199.
45   *Ibid.*, p. 200.
46   *Ibid.*, p. 84.
47   HL, p. 107.
48   GK, p. 90.
49   W, p. 56.
50   *Ibid.*, pp. 123, 117.
51   *Ibid.*, p.123.
52   *See* her *Story of A Soul*, *op. cit.*, pp. 99-100.
53   W, pp. 118-9.
54   *Ibid.*, p. 238.
55   *Ibid.*, p. 238.
56   *Ibid.*, p. 239.
57   *Ibid.*, p. 239.
58   *Ibid.*, p. 240.
59   *See* her *Story of A Soul*, *op. cit.*, p. 194.

60 GK, p. 91.
61 *See* HL, pp. 12–13.
62 *Ibid.*, p. 13.
63 W, p. 241.
64 Cf. *ibid.*, p. 241.
65 *Gedanken zur Karwoche 1938* (*Thoughts on Holy Week 1938*): GK in the bibliography of works consulted.
66 GK, p. 91.
67 Bernadette Soubirous, *Carnet de notes intimes*, Nevers, Couvent Saint-Gildard, 1983, p. 11.
68 *St. Thérèse of Lisieux: Her Last Conversations*, *op. cit.*, p. 161.
69 Raniero Cantalamessa, *Mary: Mirror of the Church*, tr. Frances Lonergan Villa, Collegeville, Minnesota, The Liturgical Press, 1992, p. 121.
70 GK, p. 88; my italics.
71 GK, p. 87. This link is also explained in *Redemptoris Mater*, # 24 and *Mulieris Dignitatem*, # 11.
72 GK, p. 88.
73 *Ibid.*, pp. 90–1.
74 GK, p. 89; tr. Joanne Mosley. An earlier version, based on an alternative German original, appeared in *Mount Carmel*, vol. 50, no. 1 (January–March 2002), p. 64.

CHAPTER SEVEN

QUEEN ESTHER: INTERCESSION AND THE JEWISH PEOPLE

Edith Stein was a person of ideals. And of ideal figures. Perhaps the first such landmark in her life was Edmund Husserl, the famous philosopher. Even when she became his assistant, she still thought of him as the 'Master' and his manuscripts as the 'holy of holies'. Giving up his work to do her own was like entering a void. One that was filled, eventually, by Teresa of Avila: a new landmark, whose books were indeed a 'holy of holies' – revealing, as they do, Jesus, the true 'Master'.

But Husserl and Teresa do not belong side by side. Edith's relationship with them was quite different. Husserl made unreasonable demands, expecting her to stifle, if need be, her own authenticity. Not so with Teresa: she brought it out. To follow Teresa was for Edith to be herself.

That is why Queen Esther is so important if we are to understand Edith. For when she tells us about Esther, she is really telling us about herself. Both were a 'sign of contradiction': a Jewess in a Gentile environment, and in some ways an outsider even to their fellow Jews. Through the figure of Esther, Edith developed a double mission: first for the Jews, then also for the Christians.

The Story of Esther

The story takes place in the Persian Empire of King Ahasuerus where the Jewish people are in exile. A wicked minister, Haman, is enraged when Mordecai, a Jew, refuses to bow down to him. Haman swears revenge – not just on Mordecai but on all the Jews. He gets the King to agree to a terrible plot: the annihilation of the Jews.

Mordecai, however, has one channel of hope: his adopted cousin Esther, whom Ahasuerus has made his Queen. Mordecai sends word: plead to the King for our safety. But Esther refuses. She is afraid, for it will mean her death. The King has a custom whereby a person may speak to him only when he holds out the golden sceptre; if even Esther goes to him without it, she will be killed. Mordecai, however, dismisses her refusal as he sees God's Providence in the situation. You, he says to Esther, have been placed at the King's court precisely for this purpose: to save your people. Esther now accepts. In trepidation she approaches the King. The plan succeeds, Haman is sentenced to death, and a new Jewish feast day is instituted: *Purim*, meaning 'lots', so called because Haman had drawn lots to decide the day of the pogrom. It is celebrated to the present day.

There are two books of Esther in the Bible: one Hebrew, the other Greek. Edith followed the Greek one. We know this from some of the details she mentions, like the terrified Esther leaning on the shoulder of her maid. Those dramatic details that so inspired the French playwright, Racine, in his *Esther* of 1689 – a three-act 'tragedy based on Scripture'. But more than detail, it was the emphasis of the Greek text that Edith followed. The Hebrew book may show Esther's persuasion as successful, but the Greek version reveals that it is God – not Esther – who wins. For Esther prays desperately; then, as she approaches without the golden sceptre, the King's face flushes with anger and God suddenly '[changes] the spirit of the king to gentleness' (15:8). To pray and to allow God to act – that was Edith's own way of life.

A Growing Awareness

Gradually, Edith grew into the person of Queen Esther. In *Life in a Jewish Family*, she looked back to the feasts that made an impression on her as a child. *Purim*, though, did not receive a mention. The Stein family probably celebrated it; but the figure of Esther had no impact on Edith at that time.

When Edith was about forty, Esther began to impinge on her awareness. She prayed in the Blessed Sacrament chapel at Beuron, where there was a picture of Esther along with other Jewish heroines: Judith and Miriam, for example. Lecturing in 1932, Edith referred to Esther and Judith as 'prefigurements of Mary' – women with a 'special mission'.[1] Esther, for Edith, was important but still one figure among others.

All that changed in 1938. Through dire political circumstances, Esther came to symbolize Edith's own mission and aspirations to help the Jewish people. It suddenly hit her with force that here were striking parallels between the Jews in Queen Esther's Persia and her own people in Nazi Germany. As Edith was to put it: 'And today another Haman / Has sworn to annihilate them in bitter hate.'[2] As soon as Hitler, this 'Haman', had come to power in 1933, Jews were threatened in every way. They were dismissed from their posts, made the target of wicked propaganda, and set on course for destruction. In 1935, the Nuremberg Laws were passed, containing the fateful clause: 'A Jew cannot be a citizen of the Reich.'[3] By these few words, the 'German Jews' were no longer 'German' – in their homeland, they were exiles. Just as Esther's people had been exiles.

And so, they took steps to emigrate. All through the year of 1938, Edith was preoccupied with what was going on among her family and friends. Some had left Germany, others were applying to leave, still more were stranded. In a heart-rending letter to her Ursuline friend, Mother Petra, Edith poured out her worries, thus reflecting the misery surely endured by all Jewish families at the time:

My brother left for the United States on October 14, just in the nick of time. His oldest son was in a camp until a few days ago, but now will probably be able to follow soon. My brother-in-law has been over there for several months seeking information; he has now received permission to remain there and to have his wife and children join him immediately . . . The Hamburg relatives are getting ready for their departure to join their son in Colombia; one daughter is going to Norway. My sisters in Breslau are the worst off.[4]

Before long, the tensions came to a head. 9 November 1938 was the infamous *Kristallnacht* or 'Night of Broken Glass'. Synagogues and Jewish properties were vandalized or razed to the ground; many Jews were driven from their homes. Throughout Germany. Organized by the State. This terrible attack revealed the Nazis' determination to crush and annihilate the Jews. Just days before, in the electric stillness preceding the storm, Edith came to identify herself totally with Queen Esther. As she wrote to Mother Petra, with the latest news of her family:

And [I also trust] in the Lord's having accepted my life for all of them. I keep having to think of Queen Esther who was taken from among her people precisely that she might represent them before the king. I am a very poor and powerless little Esther, but the King who chose me is infinitely great and merciful. That is such a great comfort.[5]

A New Esther

With these words, Edith expressed the very kernel of her mission in Carmel: it was an apostolate of prayer and sacrifice, channelled by her burning desire to help her Jewish people. Every phrase of the passage just quoted reveals something of her vocation.

I trust in the Lord's having accepted my life. Edith's life was pure offering. Even from childhood, she never hesitated to give help to anyone who needed her. In August 1914, the very moment war was declared, Edith had put down her book and volunteered to the Red Cross. Entering Carmel, she had given up everything, even her name. In this sense, God had already accepted her whole life. But Edith sensed a far greater sacrifice, like that of Maria Erzberger, the Carmelite who offered her life for Pius XI who was ill; whereas he recovered, she died the same year at the age of thirty-five.[6] That was in 1937. At the end of the following year, Edith arrived in Echt and was given the cell of this very sister. Three months later – five after her letter to Mother Petra – Edith made the formal offering of her own life. We can easily overlook the parallel with Esther: after all, she survived. But Esther believed she was destined to die for her people: this, for Edith, was an integral part of the story.

For all of them. For her family, for all the Jewish people. When in 1933 Hitler came to power, Jewish families stayed close together. The cruel irony was that Edith entered Carmel – for them – that very year, and it seemed to them like a desertion at the moment solidarity was most required.[7] Here, the affinity with Esther goes only so far: Esther, at the heart of a foreign people, was always a Jewess; Edith, at the heart of the Church, was perceived by her people as a Catholic – colluding in some way with the other side. In the stark words of her niece: 'Christianity, which Edith had chosen to embrace, was in our eyes in 1933 the religion of our persecutors.'[8]

I keep having to think of Queen Esther. These simple words are eloquent. They show the parallel between Edith and Esther not as an isolated thought, but imposing itself again and again to the point of identification. The Church, too, identifies Edith and Esther. We see this in the liturgy. When Edith was beatified and canonized, the book of Esther provided, both times, the first reading. So too does the Carmelite missal on her feast day of 9 August. As John Paul II remarked in the beatification homily:

> With God's help and by sacrificing her own life Esther rendered a key contribution toward saving her people. Today's liturgy places this more than 2,000-year-old prayer for help in the mouth of Edith Stein, a servant of God and a daughter of Israel in our century. This prayer became relevant again when here, in the heart of Europe, a new plan for the destruction of the Jews was laid out.[9]

Taken from among her people. These words take us into the theme of exile. Exile with a difference: a double exile. Being Jewish, Edith no longer belonged to Germany; and then, from the nucleus of Jewish people, she was plucked away, just like Esther: one to the court, the other to Carmel. They would *represent [their people] before the King* (we shall see this below). Let us picture Edith in the convent, snatching a few spare moments to write page after page of *Life in a Jewish Family* – bringing to life the people she loved. When the Nazis eventually seized her, Edith's exile from her people was suddenly over: 'Come, we are going for our people.'

The King who chose me. Edith's life, after her conversion, was marked by the awareness of being chosen, called. She never lost the sense of wonder and gratitude at being accepted into Carmel: 'believe me,' she wrote to a friend while waiting to enter, 'in the hours of prayer I always remember especially those who would like to be in my position.'[10]

Infinitely great and merciful. At this point, Edith could happily part company with the Esther story: God does not kill us for coming to prayer without a golden sceptre! But he may just say: if you want to save your people, then give me your life. That, too, is a work of mercy, just as he gave his own life for all of us. Like Thérèse of Lisieux, Edith emphasized God's mercy the more she herself felt powerless and dependent.

I am a very poor and powerless little Esther. 'I am' – and so we find Edith identified with Esther. In a stimulating new way. For just as Mary is the 'new Eve', so Edith is a 'new Esther', continuing the mission of the old but on a higher plane of grace. Esther is, in fact, remarkably like the Edith of old: she went to the authorities, she put in a request. As when Edith joined a society to campaign for women's suffrage. Or when she petitioned the Prussian minister to make academic posts open to women. Or again, when she wrote to Pius XI, asking him to defend Jews and Catholics against Nazism.

Now, in Carmel, Edith was a woman of 'new action': contemplative action. She already knew this as her essential role when she arrived in Cologne: 'It is not human activity that can help us,' she said at her interview in the parlour.[11] No, for what the world needs most of all is *spiritual* activity. The 'new Esther' did indeed go to 'court' – a court where the King is not on a splendid throne but in a tabernacle. The King whose 'kingdom is not from this world' (John 18:36). There, she continued the work of Queen Esther. This work is the prayer of intercession.

Intercession as Stepping and Standing

Edith loved the theatre. She often used to convey her ideas in small plays featuring famous people in dialogue: Husserl and Aquinas, St Angela and 'Mother Ursula', Ambrose and Augustine.[12] Also Queen Esther and 'Mother' Prioress (and we shall look below at *Conversation at Night*). In particular, Edith had a feel for the *physicality* of drama. She brought this quality into her prayer with great benefit and impact. It made her ideas graphic and memorable: to live 'at the Lord's hand', to stand 'at His side', to learn from him 'eye to eye'.[13]

Intercession fits perfectly into drama, like a series of stage directions. Let us not overlook Edith's definition of the role of Esther: to '*represent*' her people before the King. Two German verbs give this meaning of 'represent'. One is *vertreten*; it contains the word, *treten*, meaning 'to step'. The other is *stehen für* – literally, 'to stand for'. Edith used both terms from time to time. For her, stepping and standing made up the dynamics of intercession.

Writing in around 1932, Edith portrayed intercession as quite literally 'stepping' (*treten*):

> Even the poorest person and the one weighed down by a burden of sin can and may step in front of the Lord and pray for another person. Firstly, because the Lord is not only *just* but also *merciful*.[14]

Here is intercession's initial movement. A movement towards, and in front of, the King. Exactly like Queen Esther who went before Ahasuerus; or the character, Esther, in *Conversation at Night*: 'I *approached* the king / To plead for rescue from the deadly enemy.'[15] If we step before the Lord, we have eventually to stop before him. To *stand*. Edith used this word in the Esther letter: 'taken from among her people precisely that she might *stand for* (*stehen für*) them before the king'. It was a term so important to Edith that she used it to define her whole Carmelite call to prayer: 'To stand before the face of the living God – that is our vocation.'[16] In contemplation – and also in petition. For, as she reassured her Jewish friend, Fritz Kaufmann, alarmed to think of her disappearing out of his life: 'Whoever enters Carmel is not lost to his own, but is theirs fully for the first time; it is our vocation to stand before God for all.'[17]

Edith lived out this physical scenario from day to day. She had many visitors in Carmel – probably more than average: philosophers, religious, Jewish friends in distress. Edith listened to their worries and tried desperately to console. Then, once the meeting was over, she *stepped* out of the parlour into the chapel, *stood* (or knelt) before the tabernacle, and there *represented* these worried, anxious people before the face of God.

Like Esther, Edith 'stood for' her people in the deepest sense. More than a barrister, for example, employed for a day (or days) to speak on behalf of a client. Edith did not speak for *another* person or persons – they were not *others*, not names on a prayer list. They belonged to her, were part of her very being. Just as Jesus became one of us, and so represented us all on the Cross, Edith embodied her people in her own person. Note, though: this is not a question of race. If it were, intercession would no longer transcend all boundaries of time and space. Edith represented the Jewish people not by being Jewish herself; she represented her people – the Germans as well as the Jews, her family and friends, the Church and the wider world – because she had taken them into her heart.

Intercession as Prayer of the Heart
Edith wrote *Conversation at Night* in 1941. It was three years after her letter to Mother Petra, and Esther was even more on her mind now. Still identified with the biblical figure, she uses

Esther as her own mouthpiece. A work of fiction – but a message of truth. And this message includes a deepening vision of the prayer of intercession.

In this play, Esther appears to the astonished 'Mother', a Carmelite prioress, and presents her strange request: 'I am travelling through the world / To plead for lodgings for the homeless, / The people so scattered and trampled'.[18] These dispersed people are the Jews – so often, throughout history, exiles and migrants. But Esther's words add a new dimension. Previously, the Jewish people were described as exiled: their home was in a foreign land. Now, however, they have no home at all.

What are the 'lodgings' so badly required? Rooms within the Carmel of Echt? No, not rooms, but 'hearts' within the Carmel. 'Mother' understands and says to Esther:

... your Israel,
I'll take it up into the lodgings of my heart.
Praying secretly and sacrificing secretly,
I'll take it home to my Saviour's heart.[19]

This, then, is the new dimension to intercession. Not that it changes what Edith said before, but it shifts the focus from the *external* drama – stepping and standing – to prayer's *interior* movement: a transfer from heart to heart. When Edith stepped out of the parlour, she had welcomed her visitors into 'the lodgings of [her] heart'; then, before the tabernacle, she handed them over, taking them 'home to [her] Saviour's heart'. And so the chain would continue, Jesus handing over to the Father in turn: 'He fetches you home to his Father's kingdom.'[20] Intercession is hospitality. It is always in movement, it never stops at our door. For our hearts are only 'lodgings', temporary shelters on the path to God, our true home. It has rightly been said that without God, we will always be homeless.

The Jewish Question
While Esther was asking questions, Edith was raising issues. In her day, every statement about the Jewish people was

controversial, especially in Nazi Germany. But also in the Church worldwide. Surprising as it may seem, it took nearly two thousand years before the Church formulated its relationship to Judaism. In 1965, *Nostra Aetate* was issued – a welcome landmark. But why was nothing said before? As one authority suggests:

> the negative portrait of Judaism painted by the early Church fathers was so widely presumed by later Christians that no one thought to question what in our time has aptly been called 'the teaching of contempt'.[21]

The 'teaching of contempt' was never official. But it infiltrated the Church in insidious ways: at the grass roots, in the minds of the people. Minds that were opened to prejudice and closed to dialogue. And filled with hideously false notions like deicide: Jesus 'killed by the Jews'. In Edith's day, this teaching was part and parcel of religious education. Her own niece, now Susanne Batzdorff, came up against this sharply at the age of five or six:

> I became friends with another little girl in my class. Gretel was gentle and good-natured. One day, she met me after Religion class, dissolved in tears. When I asked the cause of her distress, she told me that she had just learned that the Jews killed Jesus. She knew that I was a Jew, and she did not want to believe that I was such a wicked person. Naïve as I was, I tried to comfort her by saying that I knew nothing about this, that neither I nor anyone in my family had ever killed anyone.[22]

From 'killers of Jesus' to 'condemned by Jesus' – an all-too-easy conclusion in the deluded popular mind, but sadly a widely held view at the time.[23] Added to this, certain Christian groups in Nazi Germany – unlike most of the clergy, it must be said – denied the relevance of the Old Testament to the New; they propagated an 'Aryan' Christianity, 'cleansed' of its Jewish elements.[24] All such views, whether ignorant or

malicious, were channelled in the same direction: to separate
Jesus and the Jews, to put an unbridgeable gulf between them.
Edith's mission was to bring them together again.

   She wrote no treatise as such on the Jewish people and religion. But in 1939, Edith translated *The Jewish Question* by
Gustav Closen, a local Jesuit priest. Unlike the propaganda,
this work spoke of Jesus as a Jew, of Christians as children of
Abraham, of the continuity of the old and new covenant.[25] As
for her own writings, *Conversation at Night* is the one that
stands out. This play contains Edith's double-faceted mission:
for the Jews and for the Catholics. For through the heroine,
Esther, we see Edith not only *asking for help for her people*
but also *educating Christian readers* on the true theological
position of the Jews. Edith was a brave woman: she dedicated
the play to Mother Antonia – she who, on first meeting Edith,
had breathed a sigh of relief: 'not a Jewish type at all'.[26]

The Jewish People and the Messiah

Esther tells her story. She begins by evoking the dramatic
scenario of Good Friday: the elements in revolt, a world in
darkness, a Cross on a barren mountain as if illuminated by
lightning. Then the liberation of Holy Saturday. Jesus comes
to Esther and her people and throws open his arms in
welcome:

> Come to me all you who have faithfully served
> The Father and lived in hope
> Of the redeemer; see, he is with you,
> He fetches you home to his Father's kingdom . . .
> We were now at our goal – in the heart of Jesus.[27]

In this vital passage, Edith is welding together the Jews and
Jesus for any minds who have separated them. She also shows
how Jews and Christians share the same path: both serve the
Father, both wait for the Messiah. In our own day, the Church
has made this last point explicit: 'the people of God of the Old
and the New Testament are tending towards a like end in the
future: the coming or return of the Messiah . . . the person of

the Messiah is not only a point of division for the people of
God but also a point of convergence'.[28]

The Jewish People and the Church

The story continues. Esther has seen Jesus face to face. She
now sees the Church – and it is descended from her people:

> I saw the church grow out of my people,
> A tenderly blooming sprig, saw that her heart was
> The unblemished, pure shoot of David.
> I saw flowing down from Jesus' heart
> The fullness of grace into the Virgin's heart.
> From there it flows to the members as the stream of life.[29]

Here Edith shows the undisputed continuity of the old and new
covenants. It unfolds throughout the Church's family tree: the
chosen people, David, Jesus, Mary, we the members. The
Vatican listed the same 'Hebrew roots of [the Catholic] faith'
in *We Remember*, published in 1998, the year Edith was
canonized. How overjoyed she would have been to read the
next words: 'the Jews are our dearly beloved brothers'.[30]

The Jewish People and Salvation

Esther now turns her attention to her people still on earth.
Travelling towards salvation. As we have seen, the salvation
of the Jews was not readily taken for granted in Edith's day.
And she too is quite blunt about their position: the chosen
people have rejected the Saviour; they are 'enemies of the
Cross'.[31] So what will happen to them? All the more, Edith
says, will Jesus and Mary attempt to win their hearts:

> The good Shepherd goes silently through the lands.
> Now and then he gathers from the depths of the abyss
> A little lamb, shelters it at his heart . . .
> But there above at the throne of grace
> The Mother ceaselessly pleads for her people.[32]

Edith was surely looking back at her own life. She had a

special relationship with the Good Shepherd who confirmed her call to Carmel in 1933 and gave her the habit on his feast day exactly a year later; and she was just as devoted to Mary whose influence she thanked for her vocation itself.[33] Through Esther, Edith is proclaiming that the Good Shepherd and his mother are seeking out their people – just as they had sought out Edith.

We think of Edith's last will and testament, with its apparently shocking statement: 'the unbelief of the Jewish people'. Shocking, that is, until we read it in the light of Romans 11, where Paul explains that the Jews will indeed be saved – a point in our own day made explicit by the Church – and that their 'unbelief' is part of God's plan for the eventual second coming.[34] In *Conversation at Night*, Edith confirms this interpretation:

> Then only when Israel has found the Lord,
> Only then when he has received his own,
> Will he come in manifest glory.
> And we must pray for this second coming.[35]

What Edith is saying is that to pray for the Jews is to pray for ourselves – to hasten the coming of the kingdom.

The Communion of Saints

When Edith took Esther as the main character in her play, it was not entirely a fiction. It was to expand our vision of the communion of saints. There is an unconscious tendency to split heaven into separate camps: Catholics in heaven praying exclusively for Catholics, and so on. But Edith uses Esther to show that all people – especially the chosen people – are joined to the mission of Mary, Queen of heaven: 'The Queen of Carmel sent you,' says 'Mother' to Esther.[36]

However, we can imagine the real Mother Antonia raising her eyebrows, struggling to accept the biblical Esther as a Catholic figure. Yet the Carmelite Order is quite *avant-garde* in this. It does indeed celebrate Old Testament 'saints', especially the Jewish 'founder' of the Order whose feast day was (and still is) 20 July, and to whom Edith and her sisters prayed: 'We who live in Carmel ... daily call on our Holy Father Elijah in prayer'.[37]

Rooted in the world, Edith nonetheless set her gaze on heaven. And so she focused on the communion of saints as the unity of the end of time, with the Queen of heaven signifying the salvation of the Jews, the salvation of all:

> We'll meet again on the great day,
> The day of manifest glory,
> When above the head of the Queen of Carmel
> The crown of stars will gleam brilliantly,
> Because the twelve tribes will have found their Lord.[38]

*

In Esther, Edith saw a saint and a martyr – a woman who offered her life for her people. This would explain why the book of Esther is included in the canon; as Emmanuel Levinas remarks about its heroine: 'The death of another individual troubles her more than her own ... It is the holiness of a book that gives [it] admittance to the Holy Scriptures.'[39]

Edith's writings on Esther have the merit of raising sensitivity towards the Jewish people – in historical events, political situations, theological truths. But Edith's message is not confined to one specific people located in time and space. We can all be an Esther or an Edith, pleading to our own King, Jesus, for every people and every person. The important thing, as Edith shows, is to carry those people in our hearts – to stand with them, and for them, before God. To belong to both God and the world, and to draw them closer together in our own person. Only then will contradiction become reconciliation.

Notes

1   W, p. 201.
2   HL, p. 131.
3   Neyer (ed.), p. 93.

4   S-P, Letter 287, p. 295.
5   *Ibid.*, Letter 281, p. 291.
6   Leuven, p. 129, n. 3; Neyer (ed.), p. 109. Edith later wrote a short biography of this sister.
7   Cf. SEL, p. 28, where Edith writes: 'What I was planning appeared to [my brother-in-law] to draw the line between myself and the Jewish people more sharply than before, and that just now, when they were so sorely oppressed.'
8   *Ibid.*, p. 108.
9   Sullivan (ed.), p. 22.
10   S-P, Letter 152, p. 154.
11   Pohl, p. 66.
12   *See* KF, pp. 1–63; HL, pp. 116–21, 122–7.
13   *See* S-P, Letter 89, p. 87; W, p. 240; S-P, Letter 103, p. 102.
14   ESW VI, p. 168; the quotation is from *The Ontic Structure of the Person*, an essay which has not been firmly dated.
15   HL, p. 130.
16   *Ibid.*, p. 1.
17   S-P, Letter 174, pp. 177–8.
18   HL, p. 131.
19   *Ibid.*, p. 133.
20   *Ibid.*, p. 132.
21   Eugene Fisher: see his 'Introduction' to Eugene J. Fisher (ed.), *Catholic Jewish Relations: Documents from the Holy See*, London, Catholic Truth Society, 1999, pp. 4–5.
22   Batzdorff, pp. 196–7.
23   Schandl, p. 111.
24   *Ibid.*, p. 97.
25   *See ibid.*, pp. 101–3, for a discussion of this work. Edith's translation was from Latin into German.
26   Leuven, p. 128.
27   HL, p. 132.
28   *Notes on the Correct Way to Present the Jews and Judaism in Preaching and Catechesis in the Roman Catholic Church (June 24, 1985)*, # 10, in Fisher (ed.), *Catholic Jewish Relations, op. cit.*, pp. 38–9.
29   HL, p. 132.
30   In Fisher (ed.), *Catholic Jewish Relations, op. cit.*, p. 70.
31   HL, pp. 92, 133.
32   *Ibid.*, p. 133.
33   GK, p. 91.

34   *See* The Pontifical Biblical Commission, *The Jewish People and their Sacred Scriptures in the Christian Bible*, Vatican City, Libreria Editrice Vaticana, 2002, # 79, pp. 181–2.
35   HL, p. 133.
36   *Ibid.*, p. 133.
37   *Ibid.*, p. 1.
38   *Ibid.*, p. 133.
39   Herbstrith (ed.), *Never Forget*, p. 79.

CHAPTER EIGHT

THE SAINTS OF CARMEL: SANCTITY FOR ALL

'She simply ran to Carmel like a child into its mother's arms.'[1] Thus spoke Raphael Walzer. He had once been Edith's spiritual director and had even opposed her desire to enter Carmel. Now he knew better, knew that her intuition had been right. Hence these words of his in hindsight, and they speak volumes. A child and a mother – they show us just why Edith was a Carmelite.

She had known other Orders – and been at home in them too. The Dominicans, to begin with, in whose convent she lived and worked for eight years. The Order's motto, *Veritas*, applies exactly to Edith. Then Walzer's own Order whose Abbey at Beuron drew her like a magnet: 'she would have made a splendid daughter of St. Benedict,' he once said.[2] Edith felt 'adopted' by the founder and in gratitude took his name, becoming Sr Benedicta.[3] But neither Order was right for her; Carmel, she explained at her interview in Cologne, was holding out something more.[4] Or she could have analysed it this way: she was affiliated to the first Order and adopted by the second. But only the third was family. Which brings to life the reassuring words of Jesus to his disciples:

> Truly I tell you, there is no one who has left house or
> brothers or sisters or mother or father or children or fields,

for my sake and for the sake of the good news, who will not receive a hundredfold now in this age – houses, brothers and sisters, mothers and children, and fields ... (Mark 10:29–30)

Carmel gave Edith just such a family, starting with its saints. They were her father and mother, her brothers and sisters.

ELIJAH: 'OUR HOLY FATHER'

Elijah, the great prophet of the Old Testament. But he is not confined there. His presence pervades the New Testament and sets in motion the Carmelite tradition. So let us look at his story; it is found in the first book of Kings.

The Story of Elijah
The background is Israel in the ninth century BC. It is the reign of King Ahab who is married to the Sidonian, Jezebel. Under her influence, the King and the people are worshipping the false god, Baal. Elijah is sent to turn the hearts of the Israelites back to the true God.

The great prophet appears suddenly and makes a dramatic announcement: 'As the Lord the God of Israel lives, before whom I stand, there shall be neither dew nor rain these years, except by my word' (17:1). This is the prelude to three main episodes in Elijah's life: before, during and after his mission. They will be directly influential on the future Carmelite Order.

Before his mission begins, Elijah needs an interior preparation. So he is sent by God to the Wadi Cherith to live in solitude, totally dependent on God. Ravens bring him bread and meat, and the prophet drinks from the stream. After a while, Elijah visits a widow in Zarephath and raises her dead son.

Once Elijah is deemed prepared and the people ready to listen, the action begins. On Mount Carmel he provokes the prophets of Baal to a challenge: to prepare a sacrifice and call down fire from heaven. Hour after hour, we see them limping around their altar, gashing themselves and wailing the name of Baal. Nothing happens. No fire. Near evening, Elijah prepares his own sacrifice and calls on God. Fire descends and sets the altar aflame. Now the people know that God is the true God. They turn back to him in their hearts and slaughter the prophets of Baal. In a scene that rounds off this stage of the story, Elijah goes up to the top of Mount Carmel to wait for rain; a small cloud appears out of the sea and we have the end of the drought. Apparently a small episode but, as we shall see, of deepest significance to the Carmelite Order.

Finally, what happens after the great successful mission? No celebrations for Elijah. He has to flee for his life, pursued by the raging Jezebel determined to avenge the killing of the false prophets. Elijah ends up on Mount Horeb where God passes before him – not in the wind, the earthquake or the fire, but in 'a sound of sheer silence' (19:12). He asks the prophet what he is doing there. The reply is now the motto on the Camelite shield: 'I have been very zealous for the Lord, the God of hosts' (19:14). Lastly, Elijah hands over to Elisha and is taken up to heaven.

Elijah and Carmel

Some parts of the Elijan story inspire a life of prayer and solitude: the retreat to Cherith, the encounter on Horeb. Others, like his spectacular mission, make Elijah an exemplar of the active life. In either case, he was an inspirational figure. Around 1190, some pilgrims established themselves as hermits on Mount Carmel near the 'fountain of Elijah'. Within a hundred years they were gone again, driven by persecution to Europe. But the story was only beginning: they became a religious Order, and the hermits from the Mount were now 'Carmelite' friars. The link with Elijah was soon made official. In the Constitutions agreed in London in 1281, the Carmelites defined themselves as successors to the prophets on Mount Carmel: Elijah and Elisha are named.[5] About fifty years later, the episode of the rain cloud entered the tradition. It was seen to symbolize Mary, to whom the Order was dedicated.[6] Edith explained this legend which draws together Mary and Elijah: 'It was [our dear Lady of Mount Carmel] who manifested herself to the prophet Elijah in the form of a little rain cloud and for whom the sons of the prophets built the first shrine on Mount Carmel.'[7]

Until the sixteenth century, the landmark figures of the Carmelite Order were Elijah and Mary. Indeed, Elijah was considered their founder. But when the Order was reformed, this focus was inevitably modified: the new, 'discalced', branch looked directly to their own founders, Teresa of Avila and John of the Cross. The Elijan strand was, and perhaps always will be, at risk of being eclipsed. For the Spanish mystics capture the imagination with their visionary creativity and large output of writings, spiritual classics in their own right. Edith Stein, however, maintained an admirable balance: straddling both the old and the new, she was a daughter of Teresa who yet emphasized Elijah as the fundamental figure of Carmel.

Relevance for Edith

Why did Edith have such a feel for Elijah? It began when she was still an agnostic, living at the time in Freiburg. Invited one day to the home of a Frau Steiger, Edith heard from her Catholic hostess about the hermits who lived on Mount Carmel in the tradition of Elijah. And Edith was captivated.[8] So Elijah – and not the *Life* of Teresa – was actually Edith's first encounter with Carmel. Another factor is that Elijah was a figure from Edith's youth. As a child, she had learnt about the great Old Testament prophet. She may even have prayed to him, for in the Jewish tradition Elijah, being taken up to heaven while still alive, lives now to intercede for the people.[9] As Edith wrote in Echt: 'Elijah comes to gather his own'.[10] She saw him as an active, living figure.

Now that Edith was a Carmelite, Elijah took on deep relevance for her life. He was someone to whom she prayed every day. A striking example of what she meant when she said that 'by becoming a Catholic she felt truly Jewish for the first time in her life'.[11] Not everyone shared her enthusiasm. Erich

Przywara, Edith's one-time mentor, was disappointed, to say the least. In fact, he was flabbergasted that an intellectual of her calibre could accept uncritically 'the legend of the founding of Carmel by Elijah'.[12] We can almost see this Jesuit philosopher cringing at the word, 'legend'! Edith anticipated this kind of reaction – she had obviously met it before:

> we revere the prophet Elijah as our leader and father. But people consider this a 'legend' that does not mean very much. We who live in Carmel and who daily call on our Holy Father Elijah in prayer know that for us he is not a shadowy figure out of the dim past. His spirit is active among us in a vital tradition and determines how we live.'[13]

This is how Edith belonged to Elijah: through a *tradition* and a *way of life*.

A Tradition

Elijah was not a founder in the conventional sense, like Francis or Benedict. Much misunderstanding has arisen in the past, precisely because of some people's misguided efforts to trace a literal succession from Elijah to the first hermits.[14] It would be just as pointless to 'prove' a lineage to the Virgin Mary whom the Carmelites considered their sister: they called themselves 'The Brothers of the Blessed Virgin Mary of Mount Carmel'. Edith described Mary as Elijah's spiritual daughter:

> the holy prophet had lived in the same spirit that also filled her from the time her earthly sojourn began. Released from everything earthly, to stand in worship in the presence of God, to love him with her whole heart, to beseech his grace for sinful people, and in atonement to substitute herself for these people, as the maidservant of the Lord to await his beckoning – this was her life.[15]

It was Edith's life, too: worship and love, prayer and atonement, doing God's will as the handmaid of the Lord. Here we see what Edith meant by 'tradition': the prophet was founder not *in fact* but *in spirit*. He was the archetype of the eremitical spirit. A spirit embodied by others from age to age. Edith found this notion quite inspirational. Even in academia, when it took the form of *perennis philosophia*. She defined this as:

> the spirit of genuine philosophy alive in every true philosopher, in anyone who cannot resist an inner need to search out the [reason] of this world ... The born philosopher brings this spirit with him into the world – as *potency*, in Thomistic terminology. The potency becomes actualized when he meets a mature philosopher, a 'teacher'. This is the way true philosophers reach out to one another over the bounds of space and time.[16]

This is why Edith could see a direct line from Aquinas to Husserl – a line of which she was a part. In the same way, she entered Carmel as one who brought with her the Elijan spirit. And who lived the Elijan way of life.

A Way of Life
Edith considered Elijah a model of monastic life. She was possibly influenced in this by the *Institution of the First Monks* (*c*.1370), a work she has referred to by name.[17] This seminal document of the Carmelite Order zooms in on Elijah's retreat to Cherith as an allegory of the ascetical life: poverty, chastity, solitude, charity. Edith, too, presents Elijah in relation to the monastic vows, but in terms of a personal calling: Elijah's and her own. We should note that although the three 'evangelical counsels' remain the same throughout the Church, they take on many forms depending on the specific vocation. The Carmelite charism is prayer and sacrifice. So it is not too surprising that whenever Edith wrote about the vows, she related them to either contemplative prayer or the Cross. Her own community renewed their vows on the feast of the Triumph of the Cross. On such occasions, she evoked Jesus as a model of poverty, chastity and obedience: his hands empty, his heart open, his will surrendered.[18] For Elijah she

followed the same procedure, this time making the focal point contemplation of God. Notably, she did not portray the prophet as the great man of action – it was not action that spoke to her most. What touched her to the core was Elijah standing before the face of God:

> He stood before God's face because this was the eternal treasure for whose sake he gave up all earthly goods [poverty] ... Elijah stands before God's face because all of his love belongs to the Lord [chastity] ... He stands before God's face like the angels before the eternal throne, awaiting God's sign, always ready to serve [obedience].[19]

Onto this monastic framework she has superimposed a specifically Carmelite value. This is what Edith, a born contemplative, noticed at once in the biblical story. When Elijah announces the drought, he mentions one phrase in passing; it can easily be missed but it stood out for Edith as if in capitals or italics: 'As the Lord ... lives, *before whom I stand*, there shall be neither dew nor rain ... '. And she was not wrong to see this as the essence of Elijah. It was a constant, reaching its climax on Mount Horeb when he again stood before the face of God. These words are by now familiar to us from the chapter on Esther. Edith, like the biblical Queen, stood before God to intercede. But when writing on the prophet, Edith captured the purely contemplative aspect: a gazing on God. It coloured how she understood one key passage of the Carmelite *Rule*:

> 'To watch in prayer' – this is to say the same thing that Elijah said with the words, 'to stand before the face of God'. Prayer is looking up into the face of the Eternal.[20]

'Holy Father Elijah'

We are now in a position to grasp just what Elijah meant for Edith. He struck a chord with her very identity. Firstly, her Jewish heritage – as an Old Testament figure, familiar to Edith from her youth. She was surely aware, too, that others perceived him as a Jew. For in an article for the general public, she quoted, no doubt provocatively, the inscription on his statue in the Vatican basilica: 'our leader and father'[21] – *Dux et Pater*. This was Nazi Germany, and Edith was proposing a Jewish figure as the *'Führer'*! In the ways of Providence, Edith entered the Order with the most Jewish connections, and they still continue to appear.[22] Starting with its roots in Elijah and its origins in the Holy Land. And then at its reform. Incredibly, both Teresa and John had Jewish ancestry – how Edith would have been overjoyed had she known this.[23] Closer to her own day, in 1862, Pius IX commissioned the Jewish convert, Hermann Cohen, to restore the Carmelites to England. And with Edith Stein, Carmel has provided the Church with the first Jewish person, since the apostolic period, to be canonized.[24]

When still a laywoman, Edith described herself as 'in longing for monastic life'[25] and especially for Carmel. Elijah, she saw, represented both aspirations – he was for her the model of the monk and the hermit. Then, she felt an affinity with martyrdom; she nourished herself on the Divine Office of the martyrs.[26] Again, Elijah was an inspiration to this future Catholic martyr. She noted that the red vestments were worn on his feast, for in the Book of Revelation he is destined to 'suffer a martyr's death'.[27] With her ultimate goal as resemblance to Christ, Elijah was also a model; he was, she wrote, 'an authentic prototype of the Saviour'.[28]

Edith had a marked ecumenical side. Before her conversion, she had visited Heidelberg and was impressed to see its 'simultaneous church' – a place in which Catholics and Protestants worshipped at the same time. Through Elijah she found once more a simultaneous worship, with the Carmelite mother house just like a simultaneous church: 'On his feast ... the monastery of our friars on Mount Carmel, the site of Elijah's grotto, is the goal of mighty bands of pilgrims. Jews, Moslems, and Christians of all denominations vie in honouring the great prophet.'[29]

Ultimately, Edith considered 'Holy Father Elijah' to be a founder in the broadest and truest sense: he contained the whole tradition in his own life and handed down the spirit through the ages. She was adamant that the discalced branch of Carmel was just that: a branch. Again and again, she presented Teresa as following the tradition of Elijah: 'Our Holy Mother strenuously denied that she was founding a new Order.'[30] Teresa she saw as reviving 'the spirit of the ancient Carmel' but giving extra emphasis to reparation and support of the Church. As for John, he seemed to Edith to embody 'the ancient eremitical spirit in its purest form'; he, too, had a new contribution: 'to be an example and to teach the reformed Carmel the spirit of Holy Father Elijah.'[31] Let us now look at how the saints of the Order continued the spirit of Carmel. We shall see how they bore fruit in Edith Stein and enriched every dimension of her life.

TERESA: 'OUR HOLY MOTHER'

Elijah the 'Holy Father', Teresa the 'Holy Mother'. Conventional titles in Carmel, but so very meaningful for Edith who related personally to the two founding figures. Think of the image of a stream: the Elijan tradition with Teresa a tributary, running parallel. These streams are traditions, a pervading presence: 'His spirit is active among us,' Edith wrote of Elijah. And of Teresa: 'her spirit continues to work among us.'[32] So let us meet Edith's 'Holy Mother' whose name she took at baptism and again in Carmel.

Who is Teresa?
Teresa was the great Spanish mystic who reformed the Carmelite Order. She lived from 1515 to 1582, and at the age of twenty-one entered the Carmelite convent of the Incarnation in her home town, Avila. Gradually, and after many inner trials, she gained deep experience of silent prayer which she came to describe as 'an intimate sharing between friends'. That sharing with God led her to see that the Order was in need of reform if the ancient spirit of Carmel was to be restored. So in 1562 she founded the convent of St Joseph's,

Avila – the first house of the Reform – and it was followed in time by many others throughout Spain. With John of the Cross whom she met in 1567, she founded the male branch of the Order. Today, there are discalced or 'Teresian' Carmelites throughout the world. Her writings on prayer are spiritual classics, especially her *Life, The Way of Perfection* and *The Interior Castle*. They are not only a rich source of her teachings on prayer but also exude her strong, profound and lively personality. Soon after Edith's conversion – that crucial turning-point in 1921 when she read Teresa's *Life* – she immersed herself in the mystic's other books. A friend who used to visit her in those days described how Edith loved the works of Teresa and would read them aloud 'as if she were praying them'.[33] In 1970, Teresa was made Doctor of the Church, the first woman (along with Catherine of Siena) to receive this title. Edith, so often ahead of her times, was already forty years earlier speaking of Teresa as a 'doctor of prayer'.[34]

The Impact on Edith

The first encounter with Teresa changed Edith's life completely. That fateful night in 1921 is commonly referred to as her 'conversion': her decision to become a Catholic. But there is more to the story. Let us see what Edith has to say about it herself:

> For almost twelve years, Carmel had been my goal; since summer 1921, when the *Life* of our Holy Mother Teresa had happened to fall into my hands and had put an end to my long search for the true faith. When on New Year's Day 1922 I received the Sacrament of Baptism, I thought that this was merely the preparation for entering the Order.[35]

This passage reveals a great deal about Edith's thinking at the time. Yes, she had discovered 'the true faith'. Yet becoming a Catholic was, we might say, only secondary – a passport with the destination, 'Carmel'. Teresa was for Edith not just a signpost pointing the way to the Church. She was a path in her own right, which Edith wanted to follow with her whole life. The impact was immeasurable. So it is not really enough to keep to the labels, 'conversion' and 'call'. We need to probe more deeply. To fathom just what was Teresa's appeal for Edith.

One thing we do know: her immediate reaction on finishing Teresa's *Life*. 'That is the truth.'[36] Edith, we saw earlier, had been searching all her life for the truth. But it was not in philosophy. It was the person of Jesus. That discovery alone was enough to direct her towards baptism. But Teresa revealed the truth to Edith in a way that satisfied *all* her longings. This is what we need to probe.

Fortunately, we have a good idea of what Edith was hoping to find in religion. She could not always put her finger on it herself, but we can read between the lines. When she wrote to Eduard Metis, a Jewish friend, she asked if he believed in a 'personal God'.[37] Judging by the curt reply, he obviously did not – but the question reveals more than the answer. Then she started attending a Protestant church. Again she was disappointed; the sermons, she said, mixed politics with religion and therefore did not reveal 'pure faith'.[38] And finally a positive experience: the visit to Frankfurt Cathedral where she saw a woman deep in prayer as if having 'an intimate conversation'.[39] So here we have all the pointers: a personal God, pure faith, intimate conversation with God. Teresa gives all this and in plenty: the person of Jesus, contact with the mysteries of God, prayer as friendship. As Edith buried herself in the *Life*, she probably could not believe her eyes. The truth was too good to be true.

And still more appealed. Edith tells us that she was impressed by the writing itself. Again, the reason is telling: if the reader accepted the truth, it was because the writer was 'truthful'. Teresa was so natural and genuine that Edith was totally convinced. So open that Edith opened up her own heart in return, to receive the gift of God:

The power of her language, the truthfulness and naturalness of her portrayal open up hearts and carry divine life into them ... Apart from the *Confessions* of St Augustine, there is really no book in world literature that bears as this one does [Teresa's *Life*] the stamp of truthfulness ... [40]

Of course, style does not come from a disembodied pen! It was the mark of Teresa's whole personality and perhaps this is what captivated Edith most of all. As she would write later: 'there are few saints as humanly near to us as our Holy Mother.'[41] Human, yes. And also near: the foundress had singled her out and called her to Carmel – where she entered as Teresa's feast day was beginning. Henceforth she would walk with Teresa 'hand in hand'.[42]

We are fortunate that Edith's account of Teresa did not end with the conversion. As a Carmelite in Cologne, she wrote three articles on her. They are a remarkable and stimulating collection, each one very different in character because intended for a different audience. Edith was writing in turn for the general public, schoolteachers and philosophers. St Paul tells us to boast in 'the cross of our Lord' (Gal. 6:14). Edith missed no opportunity to boast in the treasure of Teresa!

An Extraordinary Person

She was still a postulant when she wrote *Love for Love*. Published in February 1934, it is a short biography of Teresa written for the general public so that the Spanish saint might become better known in Germany. It is in this article that Edith explains just why she found Teresa so 'humanly near':

[Her writings] tell of the indefatigable efforts of a woman with the daring and strength of a man, revealing natural intelligence and heavenly wisdom, a deep knowledge of human nature and a rich spirit's innate sense of humour, the infinite love of a heart tender as a bride's and kind as a mother's.[43]

The phrases that appear in this impressive portrait show us a lot about Edith. She had unending admiration for the Spanish saint and applied to her the values that she, Edith, treasured

most. We can begin with *the daring and strength of a man.*
From Edith, herself a *mulier fortis*, this was a compliment
indeed. Not as a disparagement of woman's nature which in
the past has so often been dismissed as 'weak'. Elizabeth I,
Teresa's contemporary, was not exempt from pandering to
these conventions as she apologized for having 'the body of a
weak and feeble woman'. Teresa does the same, though with
a dash of her inimitable humour: 'just being a woman is
enough to have my wings fall off'.[44] Edith, however, is speaking of something quite different: a perfect balance of the male
and female characteristics present in every person. It is a
Christlike quality. And that is why, Edith said in one lecture,
'in holy women there is manly boldness'.[45] That Teresa had
the daring and strength of a man was to say that she was holy.
For holiness is wholeness.

Edith was impressed by another balance: *natural intelligence and heavenly wisdom*. The former encompasses the
knowledge of human nature and *innate sense of humour*. No
doubt she was also thinking of the pendulum between ordi-
nary and extraordinary – how in Teresa they stayed at a level,
joined together effortlessly. There is a saying that Teresa was
a mystic 'among the pots and pans'. A far cry from the Greek
philosopher Thales, whose eyes so gazed upwards that his
feet tripped up! Edith was just like Teresa: her head was in
heaven and her feet on the ground. Writing from the concentration camp, she would ask for a rosary and a toothbrush.[46]
If it were not so sad, it would be amusing. And then the final
touch of wholeness: *a heart tender as a bride's and kind as
a mother's*. These were Edith's own ideals: to be spouse of
Christ and mother of souls. She surely learnt this from
Teresa.

Throughout the work, Edith quotes liberally from Teresa's
writings on prayer. But her real aim, she says, is 'to bring into
our times also something of the spirit of this great woman who
built amazingly during a century of battles and distur-
bances.'[47] The awfulness of Nazi Germany was not so different from the Wars of Religion, that catastrophe in Western
Europe that led Teresa to found her monasteries in support of

the Church. After the pogrom of *Kristallnacht*, Edith would echo Teresa's cry: 'The world is in flames.'[48] But in *Love for Love*, Edith was content to hold out to her readers the friend who had changed her life forever.

An Expert Educator

The next year, Edith wrote an article for Catholic women teachers. Teresa was now presented as an expert educator. This work includes many of Edith's key ideas on education. The amazing thing is that they matured after she had entered Carmel and left the teaching profession. The reason for their development was that she saw her ideas embodied in the figure of Teresa. So, what are these ideas?

It all depends on making distinctions. Edith never saw education as one bland overall word. Instead, she divided it up into three different activities: teaching (*Lehren*); educating/leading (*Erziehen/Führen*); and forming (*Bildung*).[49]

'Teaching' meant for Edith mainly the imparting of facts. As such, it was not her real interest. What enthused her was personal involvement and development: the nurturing skills of a teacher, the shaping of a student. So although she knew Teresa to be a great *teacher* of prayer, Edith was interested most of all in *how* Teresa taught. Hence the title of the article: *An Exponent of the Work of Education and Forming: Teresa of Jesus*.

Firstly, education. This meant, for Edith, leading a person's will towards a goal. The goals she is talking about here – the ones that Teresa placed before the eyes of her nuns – are the ideal of the Carmelite life and the type of person corresponding to that ideal. And she could excel in the role of educator because, writes Edith with obvious admiration, she was a '*born leader*'.[50] Exactly like Elijah: another '*Führer*'! Drawing not only on Teresa's writings but also no doubt on the sound training Edith herself was receiving – for she was still a novice when she wrote this article – she goes into concrete details. Edith asks: what specific qualities did Teresa have that made her a natural leader? And she lists: a clear mind, an ardent heart, a will ready for action, a community spirit; and – here we have the most telling thing of all – *'magic power over souls* that irresistibly sweeps them along with one'.[51]

But more even than this, Edith saved her admiration for the role of 'forming': 'whereas the other activities are directed towards the human *aptitudes*, [the work of forming] penetrates to the *soul itself*, to its *substance*, so as to form it and, thereby, the whole person.'[52] Strictly speaking, she says, only God can form the soul anew but it is people who are his instruments. This takes us back to the image of the Divine Sculptor, except that now the instrument is doing the sculpting. Which is exactly how Edith saw Teresa: 'The reformer of the Order,' she writes – where 're-former' may or may not be a deliberate pun – ' . . . was a *master artist*: of that highest art for which the material is not wood or stone, but living human souls.'[53] For a moment, it is as though we are glimpsing Edith who in turn is watching Teresa at work, literally sculpting the nuns in her care. For Edith evokes a Teresa who is seeing into souls, discerning how each can follow the will of God, praying for them, and finally influencing them by the contagious effect of her own holiness: 'Holy souls are vessels of grace and through their mere contact have a sanctifying and transforming effect.'[54]

And then, rather like an artist sketching himself into the corner of a painting, Edith seems to put herself into the picture. She is one of the nuns being shaped by Teresa. For we sense the enthusiasm as she quotes (not for the first time) the words of the Augustinian, Luis de León, the contemporary of Teresa and first editor of her works. He had never met her, said Luis, yet felt he knew her well. Why? As Edith explains: 'I know her and see her continually in her living images which she has left us, I mean, her daughters in the Order and her writings.'[55] Ultimately, this was Edith's personal goal: to be a true Carmelite, a saint, a living image of Teresa. She may have been writing for teachers but she herself was the pupil – irresistibly drawn along by Teresa's 'magic power'.

Visionary of the Soul

One year later, 1936. Edith had just finished her major philosophical work, *Finite and Eternal Being*. It crosses the boundary between religion and philosophy and so, too, would the appendices. Appendix number one (which was published separately) is entitled: *The Interior Castle*. This insightful work, full of originality, is Edith's study of Teresa's book of that name, as written for philosophers.

It takes us right back to the shining-eyed student who had just discovered phenomenology – to Edith's intellectual delight as she began to analyze the human mind. She divided it up into soul and spirit and gave an account of its structure. In just the same way, we can glean something of the excitement she must have felt when she first discovered Teresa's masterpiece, *The Interior Castle*. It, too, gives the structure of the soul, but this time based on a truth that by far transcends any merely human thinking. With visionary clarity, it describes the soul as a castle made of seven concentric circles or 'mansions'. God resides at the innermost centre. The spiritual path is the journey from the outer regions to our truest centre, the place of union with God; it is the work of a lifetime.

Edith begins by giving a clear summary of Teresa's own book. But it is in the second part that we see the real originality. Edith asks a question that it would not have occurred to Teresa to ask: is there a gate, *other than prayer*, through which we may enter the soul? And she answers: yes![56] Edith now takes us along with her on a rapid tour of three hundred years of psychology. She exclaims in horror especially at one idea popular in the nineteenth century: that there could be psychology without acknowledging the soul. At this point, Edith introduces Husserl and like-minded thinkers, such as Dilthey and Brentano. None of them, she writes, seems to have entered the soul 'through the gate of prayer'. Yet no doubt because they had a religious background, they have restored the soul to modern thinking.[57]

But is that enough for reaching the very centre of the soul? Even a person of deep and persevering prayer might be in awe at the thought. Edith always believed that God was within our reach and that the answer lay with the will. For, she writes:

> The centre of the soul is the place from which the voice of the conscience can be heard, and the place of the free personal decision. Because that is so, and because free personal surrender belongs to loving union with God, for that reason the place of the free personal decision must simultaneously be the place of free union with God.[58]

Edith's conclusions are of importance not just for philosophers or agnostics seeking always to do the right thing. They are a huge encouragement for people struggling in prayer and the spiritual life. And so she sums up:

> the surrender of our will is what God demands of us all and what we are able to achieve. It is the measure of our holiness. It is at the same time the condition of mystical union, which is not in our power but is a free gift from God. That is why there is also the possibility of living from the centre of the soul, of shaping one's self and one's life, without being mystically graced.[59]

What Edith has done is to cut straight through mystical experiences and to say – in accord with Teresa, that mystically graced saint: it is *not* the extraordinary graces that matter, but doing the will of God. It is up to him if he wants to grant such graces to certain individuals; that is not our affair. Provided we have surrendered our will to him, there is nothing more that we can do. That is already holiness. And it is within our reach.

*

Teresa of Avila was for Edith as pivotal a figure as the prophet and original founder. Elijah represented her Jewish heritage, Teresa her Catholic one – with each overlapping into the other. And the Teresian tributary branched out still more,

into the various cultural and intellectual sides of Edith Stein:
philosophy of the soul, the practice of education, and – most
of all – a guide and faithful companion in an ever-troubled
world.

JOHN: 'OUR SECOND FATHER' AND BROTHER

He is 'our second father and leader', Edith once wrote when
introducing John of the Cross.[60] Yet it seems even truer to say
that he was her brother in the Order – and not only because
Teresa called him 'my son'.[61] John was destined to become
Edith's special companion as she followed the path specific to
them both: a vocation to the Cross. And this fate was sealed
by her name in Carmel: 'one cannot wish for a deliverance
from the Cross when one bears the noble title "of the
Cross".'[62] This 'title' gave her an instant affinity with John:

> [He] took the title *of the Cross* ... In the order, the title
> incorporated in one's name indicates that God wishes to
> bind the soul to himself under the sign of a particular
> mystery of faith. By changing his name, John showed that
> the cross was superimposed on his life as an emblem.[63]

But let us first look at the person himself: the 'John' and not
the 'Cross'.

Who is John?
Co-founder of the discalced Carmelites, John lived from 1542
to 1591. He was therefore much younger than Teresa but by
no means unequal. As a young man, he entered the Carmelite
Order, but the male branch was not yet reformed and did not
provide the eremitical dimension he desired. He decided his
only option was to leave and join the Carthusians. However,
Providence arranged it that he first came into contact with
Teresa who immediately saw him as the very person she was
looking for to found the discalced Carmelite friars. She later
recalled having met that day 'half a friar' – for John was slight

and not very tall! But his spiritual stature was immense. He was outstanding in holiness, totally given to prayer and penance. As the Reform was beginning to flourish, John was abducted in December 1577 and imprisoned as a 'rebel' by the non-reformed friars in Toledo. There, in the nine wretched months he spent in a dark and tiny dungeon, John conceived some of his finest verse: the fruit of intense spiritual experience and the basis of his future masterpieces, extended commentaries on the poetry. His four major works are: *The Ascent of Mount Carmel, The Dark Night of the Soul, The Spiritual Canticle* and *The Living Flame of Love*; they chart the progression of the soul, through painful purifications, towards union with God. In 1926, four years after Edith became a Catholic, John was made Doctor of the Church. For 1942, the fourth centenary of his birth – indeed, the year of her own death – Edith wrote her full-length study on John: *The Science of the Cross.* She had just put some finishing touches to this work when the SS knocked at the door.[64] John was her companion – right to the end.

A Born Saint

In Carmel, Edith got to know John's writings well. She would ponder them for her annual retreats, progressing year after year from one book to the next. That, she joked, was only in the reading of them – she was otherwise 'still way down at the foot of the mount'![65] Sometimes she included in her articles a cameo portrait of John. She never failed to admire this ideal hermit:

> We find in him the ancient eremitical spirit in its purest form. His life gives an impression as though he had no inner struggles. Just as from his earliest childhood he was under the special protection of the Mother of God, so from the time he reached the age of reason, he was drawn to rigorous penance, to solitude, to letting go of everything earthly, and to union with God.[66]

Only Teresa seems – just – to overshadow him in Edith's eyes. In her article on Teresa as educator, we find the portrait of John slightly modified. He is still 'a born saint' but there is one thing lacking: 'He was not a born leader like Teresa. He was a hermit who longed for a quiet and hidden life.'[67] Edith sensed just how much John owed to Teresa. When Edith evokes him preaching, writing and directing, she feels she is seeing 'the masterpiece which the hand of the Holy Mother, led by the Holy Spirit, has formed'.[68] That, she suspects, is why John at Duruelo knelt before Teresa and asked for her blessing.

A Science of the Cross

By Edith's last year in Carmel, she had come to a mature understanding of John's life and works. And the wonderful fruit of this process is *The Science of the Cross*. It is fully researched, yet transcends mere scholarship by its *personal* qualities: the author's empathy with John as fellow bearer of the Cross; the refusal to separate his teachings from his life; and Edith's own course rapidly heading for destruction, of which we, in hindsight, are ever-conscious.

Readers often question the work's originality. In fact, Edith might want to agree with them, for her endeavour seems to have been to let the original sources speak for themselves – hence the abundant and lengthy quotations in the work. But if she wanted to efface herself, she has not entirely succeeded! Of the three sections, the two largest are 'Doctrine of the Cross' (II) and 'Imitation of the Cross' (III).[69] The one explains John's writings, the other his adult life. Yet although Edith follows the published sources, much of herself and her own vision of John appears. The juxtaposition of parts II and III is itself eloquent: showing that John's life was consistent with his teachings, the whole rich personality surrendered to the demands of the Cross. Commenting on the works, Edith first gives her own, thought-provoking analysis of night symbolism.[70] She then goes on to show that John's imagery of the night is really all about the Cross. The night of the senses is both dusk and the way of the Cross; the night of the spirit is midnight and death; union with God is dawn and the passage from death to resurrection.[71] But it would be a

mistake to overlook the shorter opening sections: the 'Introduction' and 'Message of the Cross' (part I). This is where
Edith lays out her own vision of John's personality and
charism. In short, she tells of a 'science of the Cross'.

To understand any such 'science', Edith first goes back to
roots: to the 'science of the saints'. Here, in her 'Introduction', we sense the phenomenologist at work – seeking out
origins, defining terms before she can progress. And in so
doing, she gives a richer dimension: for a science of the
Cross can only ever be part of the overall picture; it is one
aspect – however strongly pronounced – of what it means to
be a saint.

Edith now presents us with a problem facing us all, at least
some of the time. We feel dulled and blunted, unable to appre-
ciate things according to their real worth. We want to feel
enthused by something but it so often 'leaves us cold'. Sadly,
an all-too-familiar scenario, this longing for real joy that
somehow manages to elude us. And it is especially painful,
writes Edith, in the things of religion: we know that the events
of salvation history should make a great impression on us, fill
us with strength. But they do not, and so we get depressed.
This is where John comes back on the scene.

The cure for such despondency is 'holy realism'. It means
being receptive as a child but with the insight that comes from
maturity; letting things enter us and form us. John, Edith felt,
had exactly this quality: he gave free rein to the things of religion; he did not shut them out through scruples or 'rigidity' –
and Edith's choice of word also means 'congealment'! A saint
and a 'child', John was an artist, too: he did wood carvings
and drawings, he wrote poetry. But Edith is not speaking only
about John's being an artist, being gifted; she stresses also his
artistic *nature*. And that would apply to all of us who appre-
ciate art in any genre or form. Yet, clearsighted as ever, Edith
warns against giving art an absolute value. She presents John
as the perfect corrective: an artist who not only fashioned
crucifixes but formed himself into the image of the Crucified
Christ. The Cross, Edith tells us, was the inner form of John's
soul.

Pursued by the Cross

Once Edith has established John's vocation to the Cross, she now – in 'Message of the Cross' – looks at the formative influences: the way that the Cross took root in him. What stood out for her in John's life was the Cross imposing itself on him again and again. She could not have failed to think of her own mysterious path: of how the Cross had pursued her since her birth on the Day of Atonement (the 'antecedent of Good Friday'), via the Calvary Mourning Group at Frankfurt and the encounter with Anne Reinach that revealed to her the 'divine strength' given to bearers of the Cross; up to the crucial revelation in April 1933 when she received her inner vocation to carry the Cross with the Jews. It is just this kind of life-story – one with the Cross as the title – that she sees as patterning John's own path. She begins with his childhood, with the local church where he used to see a picture of the crucified Jesus; then progresses from painted images to visions or mystical experiences of Jesus on the Cross. The first in Avila, made memorable by John's famous sketch (now popularized by Dalí's painting); the second in Segovia when John heard the voice of Jesus and made his now famous request to suffer and be despised for him.

All these influences are *particular* to the life of John. But Edith is not content to stand and stare in admiration. Every one of us has such a path to walk or story to tell. That is why Edith gives plentiful coverage to the *universal* influences: those to which we are all exposed and which manifest the centrality of the Cross. One of these is Scripture: she explores the Gospels, St Paul and Isaiah's Suffering Servant. Edith then evokes the rejected Messiah of John's poem, 'The Little Shepherd'. This glance at Jesus, movingly longing to be loved, is a point she has made before.[72] Edith was attuned to John. She was his mouthpiece, even while speaking from her own heart.

So, too, there is a blending of Edith and John when she speaks of the Mass:

> For those who, with living faith, offer or participate in the
> Mass the same thing happens in and for them that happened

on Golgotha ... We know from the accounts of [John's] life that the mere sight of a picture of the Crucified could carry him into an ecstasy. So how must the actual offering of the sacrifice have seized him ...[73]

Yes, Edith is speaking about John but also about any person ('For those who ... '). Nothing shows more clearly that *The Science of the Cross* is not a historical study about one person, but a message relevant to every reader. And especially to Edith Stein.

The 'Good News' of the Cross
With her compelling narration that evokes a sense of foreboding, Edith recounts the crisis of Toledo. She brings vividly before our eyes the arrival of John's abductors and the tense procession through the quiet parts of the town in the still of that December night. And if, for the reader, one eye is looking on Toledo, our other eye is on the Netherlands: Edith taken away by the SS, arriving hours later at a deserted railway station, and making the sad trek to Amersfoort concentration camp in the dead of night. What makes this so startling is that Edith had offered her life and expected arrest; in the final months, days and even hours, she too had one eye fixed on Toledo.

Edith evokes the captive John with the empathy of one identified with his fate. She understood how layer after layer of consolation was removed from him: no human support, torments in body and soul, being at the mercy of enemies, cut off from the Sacraments, darkness both physical and spiritual. Yet somewhere, the 'good news' – the 'joyful message' – is there, even in what seems to be abandonment by God:

Jesus can give to chosen souls some taste of this extreme bitterness. They are his most faithful friends from whom he exacts this final test of their love ... This is the great experience of the cross that took place in Toledo: extreme abandonment, and precisely in this abandonment, union with the Crucified ... Cross and night are the way to heavenly light: that is the joyful message of the cross.[74]

It had to be a fellow bearer of the Cross who could dare to say – with John – that his captors did him the greatest good. For let us never forget: Edith's 'noble title' was not simply 'the Cross'; it was '*blessed* by the Cross'. Which is why her whole book is in praise not really of John, not even of the Cross – but of the good news that it brings: 'The cross has no purpose of itself. It rises on high and points above.'[75]

THÉRÈSE: 'OUR DEAR SISTER'

Edith spoke with affection of Thérèse: she was not just a saint but 'our dear Sister'.[76] Her whole Catholic life, which began in the early 1920s, she had known of Thérèse. For in a roller-coaster drive, the French Carmelite was beatified in 1923, two years later canonized, and another two years later made patroness of the missions. Not only Edith took notice. It was the main cause, she once said, of the public's taking a sudden interest in Carmel.[77]

Who is Thérèse?

The name of Thérèse of Lisieux barely needs an introduction. She was, in the words of Pius X, 'the greatest saint of modern times'. Born in 1873, she entered Carmel at the unusually early age of fifteen and died there when only twenty-four. Despite her youth, Thérèse had a spiritual maturity that is the envy of theologians; her discoveries earned her, in 1997, the title of Doctor of the Church. She is perhaps best known for her doctrine of the 'Little Way' which has put holiness at the reach of all. It means, on the one hand, doing every small thing out of love as benefit to the Church and the whole world; it also means becoming 'little', thus allowing God's action to be all the greater. The God of Thérèse was a God of mercy – an invaluable corrective to a lingering Jansenism in the Church. Today, millions of people are flocking to venerate her relics which are on tour throughout the world.

The Impact on Edith

We do not know when Edith first read the works of Thérèse. But we do know the effect they had on her – thanks to a friend's less than favourable view! Astonished, Edith wrote back giving her own reaction to Thérèse:

> My impression was simply that there the life of a human being has been formed entirely, from first to last, only and exclusively, by the love of God. I know of nothing more sublime, and I would wish to have as much of that as possible in my own life and in the lives of all who are near to me.[78]

Edith's admiration is a salutary lesson. Many people, who feel uncomfortable with Thérèse's childlike personality and Victorian drawing room language, turn instead to Edith Stein: adult, sober, logical. Yet Edith herself found no such barriers in the French saint: she loved Thérèse. Firstly, we could say, from an *adult* point of view. With her training in phenomenology, Edith ignored outer trappings and zoomed in on the essence. She saw the radical demands of Thérèse's message and found it 'sublime'. Secondly, from the perspective of a *child*. Edith, too, had a childlike nature. Like Thérèse, she recognized spiritual childhood as an essential Gospel message: to be trusting as a child, abandoned to the will of the Father.[79] This is not a sign of weakness but of strength: Edith's own indomitable mother had a 'childlike confidence' in God.[80] The 'Little Way', wrote Edith once, is the 'path of "spiritual childhood"'.[81] Childlike, but not childish.

Edith and the 'Little Way'

When Edith called Thérèse 'our dear Sister', it was more than a term of endearment; it was a statement showing that she saw her primarily as a fellow Carmelite nun. What inspired Edith most of all was the saint's offering up of sacrifices in the day-to-day life in Carmel that is hidden and yet so fruitful. To Sr Miriam in Echt, Edith recommended Thérèse as a guide for following Jesus and Mary 'in the little details of daily life'.[82]

After all, the 'Little Way' gave meaning to Edith's own chosen life of sacrifice.

But here we see a surprising thing: in Edith's vocation of sacrifice, John and Thérèse are her brother and sister. Two completely different figures: the one austere, the other effusive. Yet Edith drew inspiration from each of them – even from their totally opposite kinds of language. Edith was true to a message's content; for her, its expression was secondary. So when she wrote about John, Edith spoke of the Cross, so imprinted on her own heart; yet when thinking of Thérèse, she wrote just as naturally about flowers instead. Thérèse famously described her making of sacrifices as 'strewing flowers' before Jesus;[83] Edith adapted the image and added her own, the fountain. Here is Edith's own account of the 'Little Way', as she was living it herself in the Carmel of Cologne:

> all the little sacrifices ... all the self-control that living in close proximity with different kinds of people continually requires and that is achieved with a loving smile; letting no opportunity go by for serving others in love ... This is the 'little way', a bouquet of insignificant little blossoms that are daily placed before the Almighty – perhaps a silent, life-long martyrdom that no one suspects and that is at the same time a source of deep peace and hearty joyousness and a fountain of grace that bubbles over everything – we do not know where it goes, and the people whom it reaches do not know from whence it comes.[84]

With these words Edith ended her article, *On the History and Spirit of Carmel*. By doing so, she put an emphasis on the 'Little Way' and the sheer greatness of its effects. Carmel's community life – the particular setting of Edith and Thérèse – may of course favour it. But the message is universal – as was confirmed when Thérèse became Doctor of the Church.

After Edith moved to Echt, she wrote a small play, *I Am Always in Your Midst*. It is marked by Thérèse's doctrine, defined here as 'the "little way" of great wisdom' – in contrast to so-called worldly wisdom. At this point in the dialogue, the character 'Saint Angela' mentions 'flowers' and 'little buds' offered up to Jesus:

> He takes them to his heart: there they bloom
> And never wither; their fragrance
> Spreads sweet and strong with wonderful healing power,
> Over all the world, closing wounds
> That people's 'mighty deeds' produce in it.[85]

In this last line comes Edith's pointed warning. No coincidence that she put her ironic inverted commas around the 'mighty deeds'. She has understood Thérèse well. For in the thinking of the 'Little Way', anything apparently great is highly suspect. It is the 'mighty deeds' that produce all the trouble in the world: power-struggles, fighting, wars. When Edith wrote this play in 1939, the world was at war. As she had said three years before, the souls hidden from the world in monasteries were the very people to help put things right: 'those homes for the interior life where souls stand before the face of God in solitude and silence in order to be quickening love in the heart of the church.'[86]

With these last seven words, Edith is quoting the essence and climax of the 'Little Way'. A year before her death, Thérèse had felt in torment, unable to reconcile her hiddenness with her desires to be priest, apostle, doctor, martyr. Then she had the crucial enlightenment: she could embrace all vocations by being 'Love in the heart of the Church'.[87] Ruth Burrows explains this timeless problem in the contemplative life: 'Carmelites have no external apostolate ... One for whom God matters supremely and who is deeply concerned for others,... will not find acceptance of this apparent non-contribution easy.'[88]

Nor did Edith find it easy. She was just such a person who wanted only to love God and her neighbour. As she heard the bombers flying over the convent at Echt, she would have thought about war and its ravages. In the last war, she had worked indefatigably, nursing and consoling the dying. Now,

Thérèse's discovery gave her everything back. She applied it to her own times and gave a fresh, battlefield reading of 'Love in the heart of the Church', where apostle and martyr are replaced by physician and nurse:

> Do you hear the anguish of the dying? . . . You cannot help here or there like the physician, the nurse, the priest. You can be at all fronts, wherever there is grief, in the power of the cross. Your compassionate love takes you every-where . . .[89]

This invisible work of the heart was truly great work. Edith wrote a follow-up letter to the friend who had so astonished her:

> [I have been thinking] first of all about what you once wrote some time ago, concerning the 'spiritual work of attention to small detail' of St Thérèse. An essential part of Carmelite life consists in this work of attention to small detail [*literally in German*: 'small work'] and it seems to me to be a very great work, a silent drilling that has the power to blast cliffs.[90]

Echoing the Whole of Thérèse

Edith's knowledge of Thérèse went far beyond the oft-quoted phrases of the 'Little Way' and 'Love in the heart of the Church'. Even a cursory glance at Edith's writings reveals that she was steeped in the works of the French saint.[91] Not just the famous autobiography, *Story of a Soul*, but the poems, prayers, letters and *Last Conversations*.

Echoes of Thérèse – her ideas and expressions – are to be found in Edith's writings throughout the years. *Love for Love*, for example, the title of Edith's short biography of Teresa of Avila, comes straight from a letter of Thérèse.[92] A phrase that meant so much to the French saint – to give Jesus joy, pleasure or delight – was given by Edith as her own aim in Carmel: 'to give the Heart of Jesus joy'.[93] Thérèse made herself small and powerless, all the more to depend on God's mercy. An inverse proportion that Edith herself adopted: 'I am a very poor and powerless little Esther, but the King who chose me is infinitely great and merciful.'[94] The attitude of receiving everything from God, of possessing neither merits nor virtues, is summed up in Thérèse's now famous phrase, 'with empty hands'.[95] Edith possibly echoed this idea: 'The vow of poverty opens one's hands so that they let go of everything they were clutching.'[96] Lastly, not echoing but quoting, Edith ended one essay in Carmel with the words Thérèse uttered the day of her death: 'I do not regret that I have given myself to love.'[97]

Ultimately, what Edith found so 'sublime' about Thérèse was the uncompromising radicality of her holiness: 'learn from her to depend on God alone'; '[her] entire life in the Order was a translation of Sacred Scripture into life.'[98] Such a life leads to death, as it did for Jesus who lived the 'word' more than anyone. His special mission – continued by the saints – brings us now to one of Edith's sentences inserted in the middle of her description, quoted earlier, of the 'Little Way': 'Finally, crowning this is the personal sacrifice that the Lord may impose on the individual soul.'[99]

In June 1895, Thérèse offered herself to 'God's Merciful Love'; she explicitly called herself 'a Victim of Holocaust'.[100] So, too, Edith offered up her own life; what she had always had in mind was '[her] own *holocaustum*'.[101] We cannot prove that Thérèse was the direct inspiration. But Edith would have felt an immediate affinity with a soul that so resembled her own. Total self-giving as a 'holocaust' – the sacrifice deemed the most absolute of all.

CARMEL'S UNIVERSAL FAMILY

With a flourish of images, Edith once tried to convey the work of Carmelite life: holiness. The resulting picture is both striking and revealing:

The walls of our monasteries enclose a narrow space. To erect the structure of holiness in it, one must dig deep and build high, must descend into the depths of the dark night of one's own nothingness in order to be raised up high into the sunlight of divine love and compassion.[102]

Why is this so telling? It is because Edith's words are full of echoes – many different echoes. The monastery's lack of space calls to mind Teresa who, like Edith, made a suggestion for getting round it: her invitation to enter the rather more spacious interior castle can be seen as an equivalent to Edith's constructions of depth and height.[103] Then comes that time-honoured phrase, 'dark night', which is almost synonymous with John of the Cross. Upon which are resonances of Thérèse's own words: 'abasing myself to the very depths of my nothingness ... Ascending once again ... flying toward the Sun of Love'.[104] Descent and ascent – again an echo of John. All this reveals that Edith was eclectic. Like the prover-bial bee of classical poetry winging its way from flower to flower, so Edith hopped from book to book. And her honey spreads far wider than any one saint.

We have seen Edith identified with the major Carmelite saints. They each brought out and enriched some part of her nature: Elijah the Jewish side, the contemplative and ecumeni-cal. Teresa the Catholic and Carmelite identity, along with Edith's strong personality, love of teaching and philosophy of the soul. John was for Edith the ideal of the hermit with a vocation to the Cross. And through Thérèse she followed the way of daily sacrifice in a radical spiritual childhood. Teresa, though, is doubtless the most pivotal figure: in Edith's life, as the cause of her conversion and call; and in historical fact, as the linchpin holding together the Carmelite saints. It was Teresa who revived the spirit of Elijah, who discovered John of the Cross, who reformed the Order out of which arose Thérèse and many others.

Let us think for a moment of the notion of 'many others'. Carmel is a tradition of saints – some of them canonized, others unknown. Edith wrote short biographies of several of these 'others'. There was, for example, Sr Marie-Aimée from a Carmel in Paris: seized by the Spirit, she refuted the writings of the famous Renan despite her own lack of learning. Then Sr Gertrudis of Echt – the Maria Erzberger we have previously met – who offered her life for the Pope and whose cell, after her rapid untimely death, was occupied by Edith. And then there was Katharina Esser, or 'Mother Franziska', foundress of Edith's convent in Cologne: when still a laywoman, she gave up her house to allow the Carmelite nuns to resettle in Germany, not knowing if they would accept her among them.[105] Just a few of the 'many others', the unofficial saints.

And this line of heroic men and women will continue. Edith was convinced that no one who lived the Carmelite way could fail to be a saint. For this reason, she even put 'the greatest saint of modern times' into perspective – as one of many others. Here is Edith's appraisal of the 'Little Way', the path of 'spiritual childhood':

> Many people came to know of this path through [Thérèse], but very few know that it is not really a new discovery, but the path onto which life in Carmel pushes us. The greatness of the young saint was that she recognized this path with ingenious deduction and that she followed it with heroic decisiveness to the end.[106]

These words show us a great deal about Edith's relationship with the saints in Carmel. For she is showing her faith not in any particular saint but in Carmel as a whole. And Carmel is far, far wider than the canonized saints, or the monasteries of enclosed nuns. There are numerous 'active' groups in the Order: the friars, apostolic sisters, and laypeople known as secular members. More widely still, Carmel embodies the countless non-Carmelites: people who do not officially belong but are nonetheless Carmelite in spirit. An outstanding example is the foundress of the Foyers of Charity, Marthe Robin, who in 1926 had three visions of Thérèse entrusting to her the continuation of her mission to the whole world. Perhaps Thomas Merton sums it up best of all: 'There is no member of the Church who does not owe something to Carmel.'[107]

Yes, Carmel is universal. It is far bigger than any of its saints. We may look to them for guidance and support, as indeed we do now to Edith Stein, a canonized Carmelite in her own right. But this is not just a looking back, it is always a looking forward. Especially forward. For the Holy Spirit is continually creative: 'this Spirit,' wrote Edith, 'that has created all traditional forms and must ever create new ones.'[108] The children of Blessed Mary of Mount Carmel – whether or not Carmelite in name – are not to be eclipsed by her, nor would she want them to be. As Thérèse once said of Mary: 'My God! How strange that would be! A mother who makes her children's glory vanish!'[109]

Notes

1 Posselt, p. 153.
2 *Ibid.*, p. 152.
3 S-P, Letter 178, p. 182.
4 *See* SEL, p. 21.
5 Technically: 'followers' of the first hermits who themselves were 'successors' to the prophets; *see* the text (known as the *Rubrica Prima*) in Wilfrid McGreal, O Carm, *At the Fountain of Elijah: The Carmelite Tradition*, London, Darton, Longman & Todd, 1999, p. 37.
6 The Marian symbolism of the cloud was first formulated by the Carmelite theologian, John Baconthorpe (d.1348): *see* McGreal, *At the Fountain of Elijah, op. cit.*, p. 45.
7 HL, p. 3.
8 Herbstrith, *Edith Stein: Jüdin und Christin*, pp. 53–5.
9 Elizabeth Ruth Obbard, *Land of Carmel: The Origins and Spirituality of the Carmelite Order*, Leominster, Gracewing, 1999, p. 79.
10 HL, p. 133.
11 SEL, p. 117.
12 Herbstrith (ed.), *Edith Stein: Ein Lebensbild*, p. 160.
13 HL, p. 1.
14 McGreal, *At the Fountain of Elijah, op. cit.*, p. 48.
15 HL, p. 3.
16 KF, pp. 7–8.
17 *See* SC, p. 19.
18 *See* HL, pp. 94–6, 102–4.

19   *Ibid.*, p. 2.
20   *Ibid.*, p. 3.
21   *Ibid.*, p. 1.
22   Note, too, the Congregation of Notre Dame de Sion (1843) and the Fathers of Sion (1854), founded by the Ratisbonne brothers, converts from Judaism, to promote true understanding between Christians and Jews.
23   On Teresa's lineage, *see* Teófanes Egido, OCD, 'The Historical Setting of St Teresa's Life', *Carmelite Studies*, 1, ed. John Sullivan, OCD, Washington, DC, ICS Publications, 1980, pp. 122–82 (see especially pp. 132–42); on John, *see* Richard P. Hardy, *The Life of St John of the Cross: Search for Nothing*, London, Darton, Longman & Todd, 1982, p. 7.
24   There is also a Jewish convert who is a 'Venerable': François Libermann (1802–1852), founder of the Society of the Immaculate Heart of Mary (1839), merged since 1848 with the Holy Ghost Fathers; my thanks to Mary Bosworth-Smith for this observation.
25   Cf. S-P, Letter 51, p. 59.
26   *Ibid.*, Letter 225, p. 235.
27   HL, p. 3; cf. Rev. 11:1–12.
28   *Ibid.*, p. 2.
29   *Ibid.*, p. 3.
30   *Ibid.*, p. 1.
31   *Ibid.*, p. 5.
32   *Ibid.*, pp. 1, 5.
33   Herbstrith, *Edith Stein: A Biography*, p. 70.
34   HL, p. 38.
35   SEL, p. 19.
36   Posselt, p. 64.
37   LJF, p. 213.
38   *Ibid.*, p. 316.
39   *Ibid.*, p. 401.
40   ESGA 16, p. 113; ESW XII, p. 191.
41   HL, p. 65.
42   *Ibid.*, p. 66.
43   *Ibid.*, p. 66.
44   *Life* 10:8, in *The Collected Works of St. Teresa of Avila*, trs. Kieran Kavanaugh, OCD and Otilio Rodriguez, OCD, Washington, DC, ICS Publications, vol. 1, 1987, p. 109.
45   W, p. 84.

46 S-P, Letter 342, p. 353.
47 HL, p. 29.
48 *Ibid.*, p. 95; cf. *The Way of Perfection* 1:5, in *The Collected Works of St. Teresa of Avila*, *op. cit.*, vol. 2, 1980, p. 43.
49 ESGA 16, p. 93.
50 *Ibid.*, p. 93.
51 *Ibid.*, pp. 93-4.
52 *Ibid.*, p. 93.
53 *Ibid.*, p. 93.
54 *Ibid.*, p. 108.
55 *Ibid.*, p. 93; *see also* this same quotation in HL, p. 65.
56 ESW VI, p. 62.
57 *Ibid.*, pp. 64-5.
58 *Ibid.*, p. 67.
59 *Ibid.*, pp. 67-8.
60 HL, p. 5.
61 ESGA 16, p. 110.
62 S-P, Letter 316, p. 327.
63 SC, p. 9.
64 Contrary to popular belief, the book is not unfinished apart from some final editing and the lack of a conclusion: *see* Fermín, *Edith Stein: Modelo*, pp. 267-70.
65 S-P, Letter 316, p. 327.
66 HL, p. 5.
67 ESGA 16, p. 110.
68 *Ibid.*, p. 111.
69 The title of part III is provided in the German edition (ESW I). In the English version, where it is untitled and the material arranged according to chapters only, parts I, II and III correspond respectively to chapters 1, 2-21 and 22-24.
70 SC, pp. 38-42.
71 *Ibid.*, pp. 46, 49, 61-4, 185. See also in these pages Edith's further nuances, especially distinguishing active and passive nights.
72 HL, pp. 95, 137.
73 SC, p. 22.
74 *Ibid.*, pp. 30-1.
75 *Ibid.*, p. 22.
76 S-P, Letter 226, p. 237.
77 HL, p. 1.
78 S-P, Letter 137, p. 137.

79   *See* MC, pp. 13–14; also, her advice to Ruth Kantorowicz in S-P, Letter 181, p. 185.

80   S-P, Letter 222, p. 230.

81   HL, p. 6.

82   *Ibid.*, p. 108.

83   *Story of A Soul, op. cit.*, p. 196.

84   HL, p. 6.

85   *Ibid.*, p. 118.

86   *Ibid.*, p. 17.

87   Cf. *Story of A Soul, op. cit.*, p. 194.

88   In her 'Carmel: A Stark Encounter with the Human Condition', *The Way Supplement*, 89 (Summer 1997), p. 103.

89   HL, p. 96.

90   ESGA 3, Letter 297, p. 29; Edith writes: 'the little St Thérèse', but only to distinguish her from the 'great' Teresa (of Avila) as the German name can refer to either.

91   A list of many of the parallel texts can be found in Didier-Marie Golay, OCD, *Sr Thérèse Bénédicte de la Croix: 'La haute sagesse de la petite voie' de Thérèse de Lisieux*, Saint-Sever-Calvados, Atelier du Carmel, cassette no. K 836.

92   HL, p. 29; *Saint Thérèse of Lisieux: General Correspondence*, tr. John Clarke, OCD, Washington, DC, ICS Publications, vol. 1, 1982, LT 108, p. 630.

93   S-P, Letter 306, p. 313; cf., for example, *Story of A Soul, op. cit.*, pp. 97, 208; *Collected Poems of St Thérèse of Lisieux*, tr. Alan Bancroft, Leominster, Gracewing, 2001, Poem 60 (PN 45), p. 192.

94   S-P, Letter 281, p. 291; cf. *Story of A Soul, op. cit.*, p. 200.

95   From her 'Act of Oblation': *see* appendix in *Story of A Soul, op. cit.*, p. 277; this phrase has become popularized by the title of Conrad De Meester's 1972 study on Thérèse.

96   HL, p. 99.

97   *Ibid.*, p. 108; cf. *St. Thérèse of Lisieux: Her Last Conversations, op. cit.*, p. 205.

98   HL, p. 108; S-P, Letter 212, pp. 218–9 (also p. 219, n. 3, showing that these words almost certainly refer to Thérèse).

99   HL, p. 6.

100 *See* appendix in *Story of A Soul, op. cit.*, p. 276.

101 S-P, Letter 52, p. 60.

102 HL, p. 6.

103 Cf. *The Interior Castle*, 'Epilogue':1, in *The Collected Works*

   of *St. Teresa of Avila*, *op. cit.*, vol. 2, 1980, p. 451.
104 *Story of A Soul*, *op. cit.*, pp. 194, 199, 200.
105 *See* HL, pp. 76–90; Neyer (ed.), p. 109; ESW XII, pp. 139–50.
106 HL, p. 6.
107 *The Ascent to Truth*, London, Hollis & Carter, 1951, p. ix.
108 HL, p. 15.
109 *St. Thérèse of Lisieux: Her Last Conversations*, *op. cit.*, p. 161.

EDITH SPEAKS

THE WAY OF PRAYER

There is always a way open to each of the faithful: the way of prayer. Whoever sincerely believes in the words 'Ask and you shall receive', is given consolation and courage to persevere in every need. Even if it is not the immediate help which, to some extent, the person conceives of and desires, help does come. (W, p. 120)

Prayer is the communication of the soul with God. God is love, and love is goodness giving itself away. It is a fullness of being that does not want to remain enclosed in itself, but rather to share itself with others, to give itself to them, and to make them happy. (HL, p. 38)

Prayer is the highest achievement of which the human spirit is capable. But it is not merely a human achievement. Prayer is a Jacob's ladder on which the human spirit ascends to God and God's grace descends to people. (HL, p. 38)

To suffer and to be happy although suffering, to have one's feet on the earth, to walk on the dirty and rough paths of this earth and yet to be enthroned with Christ at the Father's right hand, to laugh and cry with the children of this world and

*ceaselessly sing the praises of God with the choirs of angels –
this is the life of the Christian until the morning of eternity
breaks forth.* (HL, p. 93)

PRAYER AND THE CHURCH

*What could the prayer of the church be, if not great lovers
giving themselves to God who is love!* (HL, p. 15)

*Whoever surrenders unconditionally to the Lord will be chosen by
him as an instrument for building his kingdom.* (HL, pp. 14–15)

*Because my soul has left itself and entered into the divine life,
it has become great and expansive. Love burns in it like a
composed flame which the Lord has enkindled, and which
urges my soul to render love and to inflame love in others ...*
(W, p. 144)

*All authentic prayer is prayer of the church. Through every
sincere prayer something happens in the church ...* (HL, p. 15)

TIME FOR PRAYER

*One has time for so many useless things: all sorts of stupid
stuff gathered from books, newspapers and magazines; sitting
around in bars and gabbling on the street for a quarter- or
half-hour; all these are diversions which waste time and
energy like crumbs. As a challenge to the whole day, should
it not be possible to put aside a morning hour in which one is
not distracted but recollected, in which energy is not wasted
but gained?* (MC, p. 19)

*We need hours for listening silently and allowing the Word of
God to act on us until it moves us to bear fruit in an offering
of praise and an offering of action.* (HL, p. 16)

*The hours of adoration before the Highest Good, and listen-
ing for the voice of the eucharistic God, are simultaneously
'meditation on the Law of the Lord' and 'watching in prayer'.
But the highest level is reached 'when the Law is deep within
our hearts' (Ps. 40:8), when we are so united with the triune
God, whose temple we are, that his Spirit rules all we do or
omit.* (HL, p. 4)

*No human eye can see what God does in the soul during hours
of inner prayer. It is grace upon grace. And all of life's other
hours are our thanks for them.* (HL, p. 6)

REST AND SECURITY

*Each one must know, or get to know, where and how she can
find peace.* (W, p. 144)

*In the knowledge that being holds me, I rest securely. This secu-
rity, however, is not the self-assurance of one who under her
own power stands on firm ground, but rather the sweet and
blissful security of a child that is lifted up and carried by a
strong arm ... In my own being, then, I encounter another kind
of being that is not mine but that is the support and ground of my
own unsupported and groundless being.* (FEB, p. 58)

AWAKE AND ASLEEP

*Prayer is looking up into the face of the Eternal. We can do
this only when the spirit is awake in its innermost depths,
freed from all earthly occupations and pleasures that numb it.
Being awake in body does not guarantee this consciousness,
nor does the rest required by nature interfere.* (HL, pp. 3–4)

*And when night comes, and retrospect shows that everything
was patchwork and much which one had planned left undone,*

when so many things rouse shame and regret, then take all as it is, lay it in God's hands, and offer it up to Him. In this way we will be able to rest in Him, actually to rest, and to begin the new day like a new life. (W, p. 145)

WORKS CONSULTED

Note

References are contained in the notes given at the end of each chapter. For **works** _by_ **Edith Stein**, they are given with the abbreviations listed below. For **works** _on_ **Edith Stein**, the author's name is given. (Where an author has written more than one work, the short title is added.) American spellings in works by Edith Stein have been modified for publication in England. Translations of foreign-language sources are by the author.

Works by Edith Stein

LJF   _Life in a Jewish Family_ (The Collected Works of Edith Stein, I), tr. Josephine Koeppel, OCD, Washington, DC, ICS Publications, 1986.

W   _Essays on Woman_ (The Collected Works of Edith Stein, II), tr. Freda Mary Oben, Washington, DC, ICS Publications, 1996.

PE   _On the Problem of Empathy_ (The Collected Works of Edith Stein, III), tr. Waltraut Stein, Washington, DC, ICS Publications, 1989.

HL   _The Hidden Life_ (The Collected Works of Edith Stein, IV), tr. Waltraut Stein, Washington, DC, ICS Publications, 1992.

S-P   _Self-Portrait in Letters_ (The Collected Works of

	Edith Stein, V), tr. Josephine Koeppel, OCD, Washington, DC, ICS Publications, 1993.
SC	*The Science of the Cross* (The Collected Works of Edith Stein, VI), tr. Josephine Koeppel, OCD, Washington, DC, ICS Publications, 2002.
PPH	*Philosophy of Psychology and the Humanities* (The Collected Works of Edith Stein, VII), trs. Mary Catharine Baseheart and Marianne Sawicki, Washington, DC, ICS Publications, 2000.
KF	*Knowledge and Faith* (The Collected Works of Edith Stein, VIII), tr. Walter Redmond, Washington, DC, ICS Publications, 2000.
FEB	*Finite and Eternal Being* (The Collected Works of Edith Stein, IX), tr. Kurt F. Reinhardt, Washington, DC, ICS Publications, 2002.
MC	*The Mystery of Christmas: Incarnation and Humanity*, tr. Josephine Rucker, SSJ, Darlington, Darlington Carmel, 1985.
SEL	*Selected Writings*, tr. Susanne M. Batzdorff, Springfield, Illinois, Templegate, 1990.
PPC	*Phénoménologie et philosophie chrétienne*, tr. Philibert Secretan, Paris, Cerf, 1987.
OS	*Obras selectas*, tr. Francisco Javier Sancho Fermín, OCD, Burgos, Editorial Monte Carmelo, 1998.
GK	*Gedanken zur Karwoche 1938*, in Edith-Stein-Gesellschaft Deutschland, 'Wandle den Weg dem Glanze zu', pp. 87–93.
ESGA	Edith Stein Gesamtausgabe [the complete works in 25 volumes – currently in progress]
ESGA 2	*Selbstbildnis in Briefen I (1916–1933)*, Freiburg, Basle and Vienna, Herder, 2000.
ESGA 3	*Selbstbildnis in Briefen II (1933–1942)*, Freiburg, Basle and Vienna, Herder, 2000.
ESGA 4	*Selbstbildnis in Briefen III (Briefe an Roman Ingarden)*, Freiburg, Basle and Vienna, Herder, 2001.

ESGA 13   *Die Frau: Fragestellungen und Reflexionen*, Freiburg, Basle and Vienna, Herder, 2000.

ESGA 16   *Bildung und Entfaltung der Individualität: Beiträge zum christlichen Erziehungsauftrag*, Freiburg, Basle and Vienna, Herder, 2001.

ESGA 22   *Übersetzung von John Henry Newman: Briefe und Texte zur ersten Lebenshälfte (1801–1846)*, Freiburg, Basle and Vienna, Herder, 2002.

ESW   Edith Steins Werke [the collected works in 18 volumes]

ESW I   *Kreuzeswissenschaft: Studie über Joannes a Cruce*, Druten, De Maas & Waler and Freiburg, Basle and Vienna, Herder, 1983.

ESW VI   *Welt und Person: Beitrag zum christlichen Wahrheitsstreben*, Louvain, E. Nauwelaerts and Freiburg, Herder, 1962.

ESW XII   *Ganzheitliches Leben: Schriften zur religiösen Bildung*, Freiburg, Basle and Vienna, Herder, 1990.

ESW XVI   *Der Aufbau der menschlichen Person*, Freiburg, Basle and Vienna, Herder, 1994.

ESW XVIII   *Potenz und Akt: Studien zu einer Philosophie des Seins*, Freiburg, Basle and Vienna, Herder, 1998.

Works on Edith Stein

Baseheart, Mary Catharine, SCN, *Person in the World: Introduction to the Philosophy of Edith Stein*, Dordrecht, Boston and London, Kluwer Academic Publishers, 1997.

Batzdorff, Susanne M., *Aunt Edith: The Jewish Heritage of a Catholic Saint*, Springfield, Illinois, Templegate, 1998.

Brenner, Rachel Feldhay, *Writing as Resistance: Four Women Confronting the Holocaust*, University Park, Pennsylvania, The Pennsylvania State University Press, 1997.

Cargas, Harry James (ed.), *The Unnecessary Problem of Edith Stein*, Lanham, New York and London, University Press of America (Studies in the Shoah, IV), 1994.

Carmelite Studies, 4 (*Edith Stein Symposium and Teresian*

Culture), ed. John Sullivan, OCD, Washington, DC, ICS Publications, 1987.

Deselaers, Manfred, *Edith Stein – Die Botschaft vom Kreuz und Auschwitz: Zwei Vorträge*, Speyer, Edith-Stein-Gesellschaft Deutschland, 2002.

Drügemöller, Teresia Margareta, OCD, *Edith Stein im Alltag des Karmel*, Cologne, Carmel 'Maria vom Frieden', 1998.

Düren, Sabine, *Die Frau im Spannungsfeld von Emanzipation und Glaube*, Regensburg, Roderer, 1998.

Edith-Stein-Gesellschaft Deutschland, '*Wandle den Weg dem Glanze zu': Dokumentation zur Heiligsprechung von Edith Stein am 11. Oktober 1998 in Rom*, Speyer, Edith-Stein-Gesellschaft Deutschland, 1999.

Elders, Leo, SVD (ed.), *Edith Stein: Leben, Philosophie, Vollendung*, Würzburg, Naumann, 1991.

Endres, Elisabeth, *Edith Stein: Christliche Philosophin und jüdische Märtyrerin*, Munich and Zürich, Piper, 1987.

Fabrégues, Jean de, *Edith Stein: Philosopher, Carmelite Nun, Holocaust Martyr*, tr. Donald M. Antoine, Boston, Massachusetts, St Paul Books & Media, 1993.

Feldes, Joachim, *Diesen lieben Blick vergesse ich nie: Edith Stein und der Liebfrauenberg*, Speyer, Pilger, 2000.

——, *Edith Stein und Schifferstadt*, Schifferstadt, Geier, 1998.

Feldmann, Christian, *Edith Stein: Jüdin, Atheistin, Ordensfrau*, Freiburg, Basle and Vienna, Herder, 1998.

Fermín, Francisco Javier Sancho, OCD, *Edith Stein: Modelo y Maestra de Espiritualidad en la escuela del Carmelo Teresiano*, Burgos, Editorial Monte Carmelo, 1998.

——, *La Biblia con Ojos de Mujer: Edith Stein y sus claves para escuchar la Palabra*, Burgos, Editorial Monte Carmelo, 2001.

Franke, Elisabeth, *Das Wirken von Dr. Edith Stein in Breslau*, Annweiler and Essen, Plöger, 1998.

Gerl, Hanna-Barbara, *Unerbittliches Licht: Edith Stein – Philosophie, Mystik, Leben*, Mainz, Matthias-Grünewald-Verlag, 1998.

Gosebrink, Hildegard Maria, 'Wissenschaft als Gottesdienst:

Zur Bedeutung Thomas' von Aquin für Edith Stein in ihrer Speyerer Zeit (1923–1931)', in Edith-Stein-Gesellschaft Deutschland, '*Wandle den Weg dem Glanze zu*', pp. 61–78.

Graef, Hilda C., *The Scholar and the Cross: The Life and Work of Edith Stein*, London, New York and Toronto, Longmans, Green & Co, 1955.

Herbstrith, Waltraud, OCD, *Edith Stein: A Biography*, tr. Bernard Bonowitz, OCSO, San Francisco, Ignatius Press, 1992.

——, *Edith Stein: Etappen eines philosophischen Werdegangs*, Munich, Zürich and Vienna, Neue Stadt, 1997.

——, *Edith Stein: Jüdin und Christin*, Munich, Zürich and Vienna, Neue Stadt, 1998.

—— (ed.), *Denken im Dialog: Zur Philosophie Edith Steins*, Tübingen, Attempto, 1991.

—— (ed.), *Edith Stein: Ein Lebensbild in Zeugnissen und Selbstzeugnissen*, Mainz, Matthias-Grünewald-Verlag (Topos Taschenbücher), 1998.

—— (ed.), *Edith Stein: Wege zur inneren Stille*, Aschaffenburg, Kaffke, 1987.

—— (ed.), *Never Forget: Christian and Jewish Perspectives on Edith Stein*, tr. Susanne Batzdorff, Washington, DC, ICS Publications (*Carmelite Studies*, 7), 1998.

Herrmann, Maria Adele, OP, *Die Speyerer Jahre von Edith Stein: Aufzeichnungen zu ihrem 100. Geburtstag*, Speyer, Pilger, 1990.

Hughes, John, OCD, 'Edith Stein's Doctoral Thesis on Empathy and the Philosophical Climate from which it emerged', *Teresianum – Ephemerides Carmeliticae*, XXXVI (1985), fasc. II, pp. 455–84.

Jaegerschmid, Adelgundis, OSB, 'Die letzten Jahre von Edmund Husserl (1936–1938)', in Herbstrith (ed.), *Edith Stein: Wege*, pp. 223–39.

——, 'Gespräche mit Edmund Husserl (1931–1936)', in Herbstrith (ed.), *Edith Stein: Wege*, pp. 205–22.

——, 'So erlebte ich Edith Stein', in Herbstrith (ed.), *Edith Stein: Wege*, pp. 25–51.

Kavunguvalappil, Antony, *Theology of Suffering and Cross in the Life and Works of Blessed Edith Stein*, Frankfurt, Berlin, Berne, New York, Paris and Vienna, Peter Lang, 1998.

Krusenotto, Wolfram and Prégardier, Elisabeth, '*Ich sah den Heiligen Rock und erflehte mir Kraft': Edith Stein am 10. August 1933 in Trier*, Annweiler, Plöger, 1996.

Leuven, Romaeus, OCD, *Heil im Unheil: Das Leben Edith Steins – Reife und Vollendung*, Druten, De Maas & Waler and Freiburg, Basle and Vienna, Herder, 1983.

Lyne, Pat, OCDS, *Edith Stein Discovered: A Personal Portrait*, Leominster, Gracewing, 2000.

Müller, Andreas Uwe and Neyer, Maria Amata, OCD, *Edith Stein: Das Leben einer ungewöhnlichen Frau – Biographie*, Zürich and Düsseldorf, Benziger, 1998.

Neyer, Maria Amata, OCD, *Edith Stein: A Saint for our Times*, tr. Lucia Wiedenhöver, OCD, Darlington, Darlington Carmel, *c*.1975.

——, *Edith Stein: Her Life in Photos and Documents*, tr. Waltraut Stein, Washington, DC, ICS Publications, 1999.

—— (ed.), *Edith Stein: Wie ich in den Kölner Karmel kam*, Würzburg, Echter, 1994.

Oben, Freda Mary, *Edith Stein: Scholar, Feminist, Saint*, New York, Alba House, 1988.

——, *The Life and Thought of St. Edith Stein*, New York, Alba House, 2001.

[Pohl], Maria-Baptista a Spiritu Sancto, OCD, *Edith Stein, Schwester Teresia Benedicta a Cruce: Kleines Lebensbild der grossen Philosophin und Karmelitin*, Cologne, Cologne Carmel, 1962.

[Posselt], Sister Teresia de Spiritu Sancto, OCD, *Edith Stein*, trs. Cecily Hastings and Donald Nicholl, London and New York, Sheed & Ward, 1952.

Prégardier, Elisabeth and Mohr, Anne, *Passion im August (2.- 9. August 1942): Edith Stein und Gefährtinnen – Weg in Tod und Auferstehung*, Annweiler, Plöger, 1995.

Scaperlanda, María Ruiz, *Edith Stein: St. Teresa Benedicta of the Cross*, Huntington, Indiana, Our Sunday Visitor, 2001.

Schandl, Felix M., O Carm, '*Ich sah aus meinem Volk die*

Kirche wachsen!': Jüdische Bezüge und Strukturen in Leben und Werk Edith Steins (1891–1942), Sinzig, Sankt Meinrad Verlag für Theologie Christine Maria Esser, 1990.

Secretan, Philibert, *Erkenntnis und Aufstieg: Einführung in die Philosophie von Edith Stein*, Innsbruck and Vienna, Tyrolia and Würzburg, Echter, 1992.

Sullivan, John, OCD (ed.), *Holiness Befits Your House: Canonization of Edith Stein – A Documentation*, Washington, DC, ICS Publications, 2000.

ACKNOWLEDGEMENTS

We are grateful to ICS Publications for permission to reproduce copyright material:

From *The Collected Works of St. John of the Cross* translated by Kieran Kavanaugh, O.C.D. and Otilio Rodriguez, O.C.D. Copyright © 1964, 1979, 1991 by Washington Province of Discalced Carmelites ICS Publications 2131 Lincoln Road, N.E. Washington, DC 20002-1199 U.S.A. www.icspublications.org

From *Essays on Woman* by Edith Stein translated by Freda Mary Oben, Ph.D. Copyright © 1987, 1996 Washington Province of Discalced Carmelites ICS Publications 2131 Lincoln Road, N.E. Washington, DC 20002-1199 U.S.A. www.icspublications.org

From *Self-Portrait in Letters* by Edith Stein translated by Josephine Koeppel, O.C.D. Copyright © 1993 Washington Province of Discalced Carmelites ICS Publications 2131 Lincoln Road, N.E. Washington, DC 20002-1199 U.S.A. www.icspublications.org

From *Life in a Jewish Family* by Edith Stein translated by Josephine Koeppel, O.C.D. Copyright © 1986 by Washington Province of Discalced Carmelites ICS Publications 2131

From *Philosophy of Psychology and the Humanities* by Edith Stein translated by Mary Catharine Baseheart and Marianne Sawicki. Copyright © 2000 by Washington Province of Discalced Carmelites ICS Publications 2131 Lincoln Road, N.E. Washington, 20002-1199 U.S.A. www.icspublications.org

From *Knowledge and Faith* by Edith Stein translated by Walter Redmond. Copyright © 2000 by Washington Province of Discalced Carmelites ICS Publications 2131 Lincoln Road, N.E. Washington, 20002-1199 U.S.A. www.icspublications.org

From *The Science of the Cross* by Edith Stein translated by Josephine Koeppel, O.C.D. Copyright © 2003 by Washington Province of Discalced Carmelites ICS Publications 2131 Lincoln Road, N.E. Washington, 20002-1199 U.S.A. www.icspublications.org

From *Never Forget* edited by Waltraud Herbstrith, O.C.D. translated by Susanne Batzdorff. Copyright © 1998 by Washington Province of Discalced Carmelites ICS Publications 2131 Lincoln Road, N.E. Washington, 20002-1199 U.S.A. www.icspublications.org

Extracts from Edith Stein's poems, 'Ich bleibe bei euch' and 'Juxta Crucem Tecum Stare', are reproduced by kind permission of the Cologne Carmel.

Cover picture of Edith Stein, painted by Sr Marie Celeste Fadden, ocd, Discalced Carmelite Nuns, 1950 La Fond Drive, Reno NV 89509-3099, USA. Used with permission.

Lightning Source UK Ltd.
Milton Keynes UK
UKOW01f1408110416

272008UK00002B/265/P